GLOSSARY

Scottish Legal Terms and Latin Maxims
and
European Community Legal Terms

The Law Society of Scotland
Butterworths

Edinburgh   1992

Contributors

PART I: SCOTTISH LEGAL TERMS AND LATIN MAXIMS

Compilers and Redactors

ANN D SMITH BA PHD
Formerly Lecturer in Criminology
University of Edinburgh

HAMISH McN HENDERSON MA LLB
Advocate in Aberdeen
University Fellow and Formerly Senior Lecturer in Scots Law
University of Edinburgh

The late JOHN S BOYLE BL

PART II: EUROPEAN COMMUNITY LEGAL TERMS

Compiler

K P E LASOK MA LLM PHD
of the Middle Temple, Barrister

Adapted for the Stair Memorial Encyclopaedia by

D A O EDWARD CMG QC
Judge of the European Court of Justice
Honorary Professor of the University of Edinburgh
(Salvesen Professor of European Institutions 1985–89)

R C LANE BA MA PHD
Lecturer in the Europa Institute
University of Edinburgh

TEXT EDITOR

R PETER MOORE LLB
of Lincoln's Inn, Barrister

INTRODUCTION

In presenting this new Glossary it is, perhaps, appropriate first to explain what a glossary is. It is defined in the *Oxford English Dictionary* as 'a list with explanations of abstruse, antiquated, dialectal, or technical terms', and as an example of the use of the word that dictionary quotes from the *Philosophical Transactions of the Royal Society* in 1696: 'The Glossary ... is not only an Account of Words and Phrases, but also an explication of ancient Customs, Laws and Manners'.

Part I

The Glossary is divided into two parts. Part I contains general Scottish legal terms and Latin maxims which are found in the context of Scots law.

What is attempted in Part I is a succinct explanation of words and phrases used by Scots lawyers the meanings of which might not be immediately apparent to those coming across those words and phrases, be they students, lawyers from other jurisdictions, members of the public, or even Scots lawyers themselves. If some of the entries seem to the Scots lawyer too obvious to require explanation it must be remembered that to the reader furth of Scotland such terms as 'hamesucken', 'multiplepoinding', 'spuilzie' and 'falsing the doom' are likely to be completely meaningless, and one at least of them he would almost certainly mispronounce.

Inevitably Part I of the Glossary contains a large number of words and phrases which are no longer in common use. Their inclusion is, however, necessary because they will be found in old books, reports and statutes, and the modern reader may not understand what is being said unless the obsolete terms are explained. Obsolescence is itself an unreliable quality, as the term 'stouthrief' shows. In 1797 Hume wrote that robbery 'formerly passed under the name of *stouthrief*', and in 1967 Sheriff Gordon described the term as 'now in desuetude', yet it reappeared, without explanation, in section 285 of the Criminal Procedure (Scotland) Act 1975.

A large number of Latin words and phrases have been included. The importance of Roman law as a source of Scots law is demonstrated by the continuing frequent use of Latin by Scots lawyers, which unfortunately is accompanied by the gradual erosion of classical studies from contemporary education. It is consequently increasingly necessary to have to hand an explanation of the meaning of words and phrases which will be constantly met in legal practice.

Legal language does not stand still. With the growing complexity of modern life new concepts continue to arise with new terminologies. In the field of town and country planning, for example, there is a plethora of terms in constant use which did not exist a century ago. We have hesitated to include more than a few such terms because their meanings are either self-evident or are explained in the relevant statutes. Nevertheless many words and phrases are included which were unknown when earlier Scots lawdictionaries were written.

By and large statutory definitions have not been added to this Glossary, for five reasons. First, statutory definitions apply only to the statutes in which they appear. Secondly, they are generally artificial meanings, in the sense that the words defined are used in the particular Act not with their ordinary meanings but rather as concise ways of expressing what otherwise would require a lengthy explanation each time they were used (an example is ' "land" includes land covered by water'). Thirdly, because Acts are readily available, statutory definitions are always to hand. Fourthly, the same words may have different definitions in different Acts. Fifthly, there are so many statutory definitions that to include them would expand a glossary to an unreasonable and unhelpful size.

Part II

Part II of the Glossary contains terms used in European Community law, and is adapted, by the generous permission of its compiler, Mr K P E Lasok, from the glossary which he prepared in 1985 for the EUROPEAN COMMUNITIES title of *Halsbury's Laws of England*.

PART I: SCOTTISH LEGAL TERMS AND LATIN MAXIMS

a

a coelo usque ad centrum — from the sky to the centre of the earth. This description of the scope of ownership of land was formerly generally accepted but has now been qualified by planning and other legislation.

a fortiori — by a stronger argument: a phrase used to emphasise the strength of an argument by contrasting it with an earlier weaker proposition founded on the same or similar reasoning.

a mensa et thoro — from bed and board; judicial separation of husband and wife.

a morte testatoris — from the death of the testator: a phrase distinguishing bequests which vest upon a testator's death from those where vesting is postponed to a later date.

a non domino — from one who is not the owner: used to describe a title given by one who does not pretend to be the owner, as when land is sold by a lawful occupier when all trace of the identity of the true owner has been lost. The purchaser's defective title is cured by prescription.

a posteriori — viewed from after; reasoning from effect to cause.

a priori — viewed from before — reasoning from cause to effect.

a vinculo matrimonii — from the bond of marriage; divorce, permitting remarriage.

ab initio — from the beginning. Thus a bigamous marriage is said to be void *ab initio*.

ab intestato — from a person dying intestate; description of property acquired according to the rules of intestate succession.

abbreviate — an abstract of a writ and warrant recorded in an official register in bankruptcy proceedings to give public notice thereof.

absolute discharge — an order which may be made by a court instead of imposing a sentence when the court has found a person guilty of a crime or offence but considers that any punishment would be inappropriate. An offender cannot receive an absolute discharge if the penalty is fixed by statute. A court of summary jurisdiction may make the order without the offender being convicted, but may also order an absolute discharge after conviction. When an offender is tried and convicted on indictment, the conviction is always recorded.

absolute warrandice — *See* **warrandice.**

absolutely insolvent — the state of a debtor whose liabilities are greater than his assets.

absolvitor — a final civil judgment in favour of the defender. *See* **assoilzie.**

abstract — a summary of a document.

acceptilatio or **acceptilation** — the discharge of an obligation by complete or partial remission of performance.

access — the rights conferred by a court on the parent or other relative who is not given the right of custody of a child under sixteen. This right may include the opportunity to have the child to stay or to visit for a stated period. A court may refuse access if it considers this to be in the child's interest.

accession —

(1) the natural or industrial (qv) accretion of additional objects to existing property (eg by reproduction or building);

(2) an arrangement set out in a deed approved by the creditors of an insolvent person as an alternative to sequestration.

accessorium principale sequitur — the accessory follows the principal thing to which it is attached. Thus the owner of land owns buildings attached to it and its fruits, and the owner of cattle has a right to their offspring.

accessory — a person who aids or advises the perpetrator of a crime. Cf **art and part.**

accessory action — an action intended to achieve some further procedural objective. Such an action involves eg proving the tenor (qv) so as to base a claim for a later action.

accessory obligation — an obligation imposed to increase the effectiveness of an earlier obligation, eg caution.

accidentalia — accidents: incidental, as contrasted with essential, parts of a contract.

account charge and discharge — a form of account of transactions of property committed to the care of trustees, executors, factors etc or their agents. The account is generally drawn up annually and deals with credits, debits and capital in hand.

Accountant in Bankruptcy — the Accountant of Court in his capacity as the officer supervising the administration of sequestration (bankruptcy) and personal insolvency.

Accountant of Court — the officer of the Court of Session supervising the conduct of judicial factors and certain tutors and curators.

accretion —
  (1) the passing of the share of a deceased joint legatee to the other joint legatee or legatees;
  (2) in the case of a conveyance of title to heritable property, the perfection of a formerly imperfect title of the granter may cause validation of the grantee's title by accretion;
  (3) *alluvio* (qv).

accused — a person charged with committing a crime or offence. *See also* **panel.**

acquiescence — a personal bar which arises through failure by a person whose rights have been infringed to object within the time allowed, proof of knowledge of the acts done being essential to infer consent.

acquisita et acquirenda — things acquired and to be acquired, relevant in the execution of diligence and the law of bankruptcy.

act and warrant — in sequestration, a judicial order confirming the appointment of a permanent trustee in terms of the Bankruptcy Act 1985.

Act of God. *See damnum fatale.*

actings — conduct or acts.

actio injuriarum — a Roman action for penal damages to vindicate offensive behaviour. In Scots law the phrase has been correctly applied to an action for affront (qv) and more recently but incorrectly, though with judicial recognition, to an action for *solatium* for the death of a relative, now replaced by a loss of society award (qv).

actio quanti minoris — an action in Roman law whereby the purchaser of goods could retain them and seek from the seller the difference between their actual value and the value they should have had under the contract. The action was not in general recognised by the common law of Scotland but was effectively introduced into Scots law by section 11 of the Sale of Goods Act 1893.

action — civil (but not criminal) proceedings to obtain from the court some civil remedy of advantage to the pursuer.

actor debet sequi forum rei — a pursuer must follow the court of the defender. Thus jurisdiction is normally determined by the residence of the defender.

Acts of Adjournal — rules made by the High Court of Justiciary regulating procedure there and in inferior criminal courts, published as statutory instruments.

Acts of Sederunt — rules made by the Court of Session regulating procedure in the Court of Session, the sheriff court (in non-criminal matters) and administrative tribunals, usually published as statutory instruments.

actus non facit reum, nisi mens sit rea — an act does not infer criminality unless the actor had criminal intent or criminal negligence. This maxim is usually now simply expressed in references to *mens rea* (qv).

actus reus — the physical act or conduct prohibited in a crime or offence.

ad civilem effectum — as to the civil effect, contrasted with effect in criminal law. An activity may have separate civil and criminal effects.

ad factum praestandum — for the performance of an act. In modern practice a decree or an obligation *ad factum praestandum* requires the performance or fulfilment of some physical rather than pecuniary obligation.

ad fundandam jurisdictionem — for the purpose of founding jurisdiction.

ad interim — in the meantime.

ad litem — as regards the action. Thus a curator *ad litem* is a curator appointed for the purposes of a specific action to look after the interests of a party under legal disability.

ad longum — at length, used of documents or statements in contrast to a precis or summary.

ad medium filum — to the middle line, normally used of the rights of proprietors of opposite banks of a river.

ad omissa vel male appretiata — as regards things omitted or undervalued, in the context of a confirmation and inventory submitted by executors.

ad valorem — according to value; proportionally, as of stamp duties.

ad vindictam publicam — for the maintenance and defence of the public interest: the particular concern of the Lord Advocate and procurators fiscal as public prosecutors.

ad vitam aut culpam — for life or until fault is established; formerly included in the terms of appointment to certain public offices such as judges and professors of law; now mostly superseded by specific contracts or by statutory retirement ages.

ademptione — by ademption. Specific legacies are revoked by ademption when the thing bequeathed has ceased to exist or has been disposed of by the testator before the time of death.

adhere —
(1) by a court, to confirm the judgment given by a lower court;
(2) by a husband or wife, to cohabit at bed and board (the action to secure adherence was abolished in 1984).

adjudication —
(1) (generally) judicial determination;
(2) the means by which the Court of Session vests a title to land in a claimant entitled thereto or attaches the heritable property of a debtor in security or in satisfaction of a debt (*see also* **foreclosure; poind**);
(3) a decision on stamp duties made by the Inland Revenue Commissioners.

adjust — to alter written pleadings in a civil action before the court closes the record.

adjustment roll. *See* **rolls.**

adminicle — an item of helpful evidence.

administration order — an order made under a procedure introduced by Part II of the Insolvency Act 1986 (ss 8–27) which is designed to secure the rehabilitation of an ailing company or the better realisation of its assets than would follow upon a formal winding up of the company.

administrator — a person appointed by the court to manage the affairs of a company under an administration order (qv).

administrator at (*or* in) law — a title of a parent as the tutor of a pupil child or the curator of a minor child. At common law the father is natural guardian or administrator in law of his legitimate child while in minority, and consequently tutor to his pupil and curator to his minor child. The Guardianship Act 1973 gave the mother in all cases equal rights of guardianship with the father. The position of administrator at law is not strictly an office but is inseparable from relationship.

admissible evidence — testimony given to a court or tribunal which conforms with the law of evidence in respect of competency and relevance.

admonition — a form of disposal by a court, in criminal cases, after an offender has been found guilty, where the court considers that a censure or warning would be a more appropriate means of dealing with the accused than the imposition of a greater punishment.

adopted as holograph — a phrase written by the subscriber to a deed immediately above his signature which implies his acceptance of the deed as though it were handwritten by him throughout. Witnesses to his signature are then unnecessary.

adoption—
(1) the acceptance as valid of a document which would otherwise be defective on grounds of informality (*see also* **adopted as holograph**);
(2) the vesting of parental rights and duties in an individual when those of the natural parents are extinguished.

advise — to give judgment after having taken time for consideration. *See also avizandum.*

advocate —
(1) a member of the Scottish Bar;
(2) a solicitor who is a member of the Society of Advocates in Aberdeen.
(3) to submit the judgment of an inferior court for review. In modern practice this procedure is rare and is restricted to criminal jurisdiction.

Advocate Depute — an advocate appointed by the Lord Advocate to act as Crown counsel and to assist or represent him in the prosecution of crime.

advocation — an old form of appeal to a superior court. It now survives only in criminal procedure where it is occasionally used by the Crown to bring irregularities in an inferior court before the High Court of Justiciary. It proceeds upon a writ known as a bill (qv).

aedificatum solo, solo cedit — what is built upon the ground accrues to it.

aemulatio vicini — the purpose of annoying or injuring a neighbour, a motive which may render unlawful an otherwise lawful act.

affidavit — a written statement made on oath and signed, hitherto rarely used in Scotland but now in general use in undefended actions for divorce.

affiliation *or* **filiation** — an action raised to determine the paternity of a child, usually an illegitimate child.

affirm — to declare solemnly as a witness the truth of one's evidence when one objects to taking an oath. In practice the form of words is 'I solemnly, sincerely and truly declare and affirm that I will tell the truth, the whole truth and nothing but the truth'.

affront — insulting or threatening words or conduct.

agent — a person authorised expressly or by implication to act on behalf of another. *See also* **law agent; principal.**

agent disburser — a solicitor who has advanced or incurred the costs of an action and who may be entitled to seek in his own name a decree for the expenses awarded to his client.

aggravation — a circumstance in a criminal case which adds to the seriousness of the case, eg the existence of a previous conviction, or the circumstances or purpose of an assault.

agnate — a person related to another on the father's side, as distinct from a cognate, who is related on the mother's side.

alias — an assumed or alternative name, usually assumed for criminal purposes.

alibi — elsewhere: a defence to a criminal charge that the accused was not at the *locus* of the crime but at some other specified place.

aliment — provision for maintenance for the support of a spouse or child. Formerly the law recognised a mutual obligation of support between ancestors and dependants. See now the Family Law (Scotland) Act 1985, ss 1–7.

alimentary — (as a description of a fund) not available to meet the claims of creditors, eg alimentary liferent. Formerly common in antenuptial contracts of marriage where property was provided by the wife; since 1984 the privilege may extend only to funds provided by third persons.

aliud est celare, aliud tacere — it is one thing to conceal, another to remain silent: Cicero, *De Officiis*. Thus a seller in some situations may remain silent, but must not conceal defects.

aliunde — otherwise, or from some other source or direction. Eg certain contractual obligations may be proved only by writ or oath when more than the relevant statutory period had elapsed after it fell due; before then it could be proved *aliunde* in any lawful manner.

allenarly (adv)— only; solely; exclusively. Usually applied in cases of liferent to emphasise the restriction of an interest, preventing its being construed as a fee.

allodial (adj) — applied to absolute land tenure (eg church property, property acquired
by compulsory purchase and property in udal tenure) in contradistinction to feudal
property held of a feudal superior.

allotment —
 (1) a plot of land let by a local authority for cultivation;
 (2) the allocation of shares in a company.

alluvio — alluvion, the gradual accretion of new land by the deposit of sand and earth
through the action of the sea or river to the benefit of the owner of land to which it
becomes attached.

alterum non laedere — to harm no one: a basic legal principle or duty.

altius non tollendi — of not raising higher, a servitude preventing an owner of ground
from erecting buildings beyond a certain height.

amand — a financial penalty: an obsolete term traditionally applied to the payment of an
award of expenses as a condition precedent to further procedure or proceedings.

amend — to alter the written pleadings in an action, by leave of the court, after the record
is closed, or to alter the instance, crave or conclusions at any time. Cf **adjust.**

amerce — to assess a financial penalty: an obsolescent term now usually found only in
proceedings for contempt of court.

amicus curiae — a friend of the court; one who argues at the request or with the leave of
the court for an unrepresented party or in the public interest.

animo donandi — with the intention of giving as a gift, rarely presumed by the law except
as between husband and wife.

animo et facto — by act and intention: factors determining the acquisition of a domicile of
choice or the possession of some thing, in contrast with its custody.

animo injuriandi — with the intention of harming or insulting.

animo remanendi — with the intention of remaining; where domicile is in issue, used to
indicate the intention of creating a permanent residence.

animo revertendi — with the intention of returning, as of domesticated animals, pigeons
in a dovecot etc, of whom ownership is not lost by their merely temporary absence
because they are presumed to intend to return to their accustomed habitations.

annual rent — interest on money. To evade pre-Reformation prohibitions on lending at
interest lenders contracted to receive a yearly rent from land, thus 'annual rent' became
synonymous with 'interest'.

annuity — a right to a yearly payment of money.

answer — a written pleading given to a court in replication to the written claim of a
pursuer.

ante litem motam — before an action is raised.

ante omnia — before everything; before anything else.

apocha trium annorum — receipt for three years: a presumption arising from the
discharge or formal receipt of three consecutive periodical (though not necessarily
annual) payments that all similar prior payments have been made.

apparent heir — prior to 1964, the person to whom succession to heritable property had
actually opened by the death of the ancestor, but who had not yet completed title.
Cf **heir-apparent.**

apparent insolvency — the circumstances, replacing the concept of notour bankruptcy,
which must be established under the Bankruptcy (Scotland) Act 1985 (see s 7) as a
prerequisite to the initiation of sequestration proceedings by creditors.

appearance — a step taken or notice given by the defender in a civil action indicating that
he proposes to defend the action.

appellant — a person appealing to a higher court from the decision of a lower court (eg in
a criminal case from the sheriff court or district court to the High Court of Justiciary, or
in a civil case from the Court of Session to the House of Lords).

apportion — to divide property or rights into appropriate shares as between those
entitled, eg as between liferenter and fiar.

appraiser — in poinding, the person entrusted with the valuation of goods.

apprehend — to arrest.

approbate and reprobate — to take advantage of one part of a deed and reject the rest. This is forbidden by law. A deed must be accepted or rejected as a whole.

apud acta — among the acts, referring to orders judicially pronounced in open court in the presence of the parties and which must be obeyed without further notice.

aquaeductus — the rural servitude of aqueduct conferring on the owner of the dominant tenement the right to convey water through the servient tenement by pipes or canals.

aquaehaustus — a rural servitude conferring on the owner of the dominant tenement the right to water cattle on the servient tenement.

arbiter — a person appointed to adjudicate outside the courts in a dispute. On a question of fact, his decision is final; on a question of law, unless otherwise agreed, he may (on the application of either party) and must (if the Court of Session so directs) state a case for the court's opinion on the question of law.

arles — a small sum of money or small part of a commodity given as an earnest (arrhae) or token of the completion of a bargain.

arrestment — the taking or attachment of the property of another which is in the hands of a third party to obtain security against a debtor or to found jurisdiction against a defender.

arrhae — earnest: see **arles.**

art and part — in the capacity of accessory or accomplice in relation to a criminal act.

articles — clauses, paragraphs or sections of a legal document.

articles of association — management regulations of a registered company.

articles of roup — conditions of the contract prescribed for a public auction, especially of land.

artificial person — a person (other than a natural person) to which juristic identity is given by law.

as accords — agreeable or conformable to law.

ascendant — kin to a deceased person from a previous generation, eg parent or great-uncle.

ascription — the application of payments to particular debts.

assessor —
  (1) a person with specialised knowledge relevant to the subject matter of an action who assists a judge;
  (2) in local government, a person who assesses the annual value of property for rating purposes.

assignation —
  (1) act of transferring rights to incorporeal moveable property;
  (2) the document transferring such rights.

assignatus utitur jure auctoris — an assignee exercises the right of his cedent, and no more.

assize —
  (1) the sittings of a court;
  (2) a jury.

associate — in the law of bankruptcy and insolvency, a person within certain categories of relationship with another person: see the Bankruptcy (Scotland) Act 1985, s 74, and the Insolvency Act 1986, s 435.

assoilzie (pronounced 'a-soil(y)i') — to absolve; to decide finally a civil action in favour of the defender. The judgment is termed 'absolvitor'. In a criminal case when the panel is acquitted, he is 'assoilzied *simpliciter*'.

assume — to adopt eg an additional trustee or a partner.

assythment — an obsolete claim for compensation for injury to feelings formerly made by relatives of a person killed by the defender's criminal act. It was abolished by the Damages (Scotland) Act 1976, s 8.

at will — as of a contract (eg partnership or tenancy) terminable by either party on reasonable notice, as contrasted with terminable on the expiry of a fixed term.

attestation — the authentication of a deed or other instrument by the signatures and designations of witnesses before whom the granter signed or to whom he acknowledged his signature.

attorney — a person acting under the authority of a power of attorney.

attour — besides; as well as; over and above.

auctor in rem suam — one who acts in his own interest. Trustees and agents may not so act.

audi alteram partem — hear the other side: the rule of natural justice that no decision should be reached by a court or tribunal until all parties have been given an opportunity to be heard.

Auditor of Court — the court officer or other person responsible for the examination and taxation of accounts in the Court of Session or a sheriff court.

augmentation — an increase in the payment of periodic sums, eg rent or stipend.

authentication — features establishing the validity of a deed, eg the signatures of witnesses.

author — a person from whom title is derived.

authority — a judicial decision, authoritative textbook or statute justifying a proposition or statement of law.

averment — a statement of fact made (usually in written pleadings) which the party making it asserts that he can prove.

avizandum — to be looked into or considered: the taking of time for consideration before a judgment is given.

avoid — to reduce or set aside a contract.

avulsio — the violent severance of land by the action of a river, eg by flood or where the river changes its course, having no effect on rights of property.

award — the decision of a tribunal or arbiter; more rarely, the ruling of a court.

b

back; back up —
(1) to indorse details (eg name and type of deed) on the back of a folded document;
(2) to indorse a warrant so as to permit its execution outwith the original jurisdiction.

back bond; back letter — an agreement in the form of a letter, qualifying the provisions of another document that is unqualified, eg a standard security, and formerly an *ex facie* absolute disposition (which is obsolescent since 1970).

backhand rent — rent agreed to be paid in arrear, ie after the period of the lease to which it relates, as distinct from forehand rent (qv).

bail — security for the release of a person charged with a crime or an offence on conditions designed to ensure that he appears before the court: see the Bail (Scotland) Act 1980.

bailie —
(1) prior to the reorganisation of local government in 1975, a magistrate in a Scottish burgh;
(2) formerly the representative of the superior who appeared on the ground to grant infeftment in feudal conveyances;
(3) formerly an officer of a barony or regality;
(4) there is still a Bailie of the Abbey of Holyrood, the precinct of the royal palace.

bairns' part — the part of the moveable estate of a deceased person to which his issue, natural or adopted, have a legal right. *See* **legitim**.

bankruptcy. *See* **sequestration**.

Bar —

(1) the members of the Faculty of Advocates in Scotland;

(2) solicitors practising in a local court, eg members of the Glasgow Bar Association.

bar of trial. *See* **plea in bar of trial**.

barony — a direct grant of an estate in land from the Crown; few benefits remain, and the privileges in the form of civil and criminal jurisdiction are obsolete.

base holding — a holding, under the feudal system of land tenure, from a person who does not hold directly from the Crown but whose holding has been subfeued from an original superior holder.

before answer — *See* **proof before answer**.

behoof — advantage; benefit.

benefice — the living or provision for a minister of a parish.

beneficiary — a person who will benefit from the terms of a deed such as a will or a trust instrument.

beneficium — a right, privilege or benefit.

beneficium competentiae — the right of a bankrupt to retain from his estate sufficient funds for his own maintenance; and the similar right of a person who is liable to aliment dependants.

beneficium discussionis — the right of a cautioner that all co-cautioners should share the obligation *pro rata*.

beneficium ordinis — benefit of discussion, the right of a debtor to insist that the creditor proceed first against the principal debtor.

bill —

(1) a form of procedure now used only in certain proceedings in the Court of Session or the High Court of Justiciary;

(2) a document asserting an obligation for the payment of money on a debt;

(3) provisions presented to Parliament for the purpose of being passed into law as a statute.

Bill Chamber — a former department of the Court of Session, with responsibility among other things for proceedings begun by bill, now called the Petition Department.

billet — an order requiring the occupier of premises to provide accommodation for members of HM forces or their vehicles.

blackmail — the extortion of money by the use of illegal force or threats. Originally it was an annual extortion paid to armed bands for 'protection'.

blanch — *see* **blench**.

blank bond — a bond, long since invalidated by statute, containing a blank in place of the creditor's name, and which accordingly circulated as a bearer bond.

blench *or* **blanch** — a feudal holding where the feuduty takes only a nominal form, eg one penny Scots, if asked only.

blood relationship — the relationship between two people who have either one common parent (relationship of the half blood) or two common parents (relationship of the whole blood), as distinguished from relationship by marriage, where no parent is shared.

blood test —

(1) a test on a sample of blood to determine whether the alcohol level exceeds the limit prescribed under road traffic legislation;

(2) a test on a sample of blood to determine whether paternity can be excluded.

boll — a measure of grain or pulse. 16 bolls amount to a chalder.

bona fide — in good faith, acting honestly, even if negligently or mistakenly, or even foolishly, but not fraudulently or deceptively or without inquiry where reasonable suspicion is raised.

bona fide perceptio et consumptio — gathering and consumption of crops in good faith by persons having an apparently good but in fact defective title.

bona fides — good faith. *See* *bona fide*.

bona vacantia — property of persons dying without successors, and other ownerless property, which falls to the Crown and is administered by the Crown Agent who has taken over the functions of the Queen's and Lord Treasurer's Remembrancer.

bond — a written obligation to pay money or to do or refrain from doing an act. Until replaced by the standard security in 1970, the bond and disposition in security was the normal form of securing a debt with heritable property.

bond of corroboration — in conveyancing, an additional obligation granted by the debtor in a bond by which he corroborates the original obligation.

booking — a form of land tenure in the Burgh of Paisley under which rights were secured by registration in the Register of Booking, and now secured by registration in the Land Register of Scotland.

Books of Adjournal — the records of the High Court of Justiciary.

Books of Council and Session — the Registers of Deeds and Probative Writs, kept by the Keeper of the Registers of Scotland, in which a wide variety of deeds may be registered.

Books of Sederunt — records kept by the Court of Session in which Acts of Sederunt require to be inserted.

border warrant — an obsolete form of warrant for the arrest of the effects and person of someone in England for debts owed in Scotland.

bounding charter; bounding title — a deed which defines the land comprised in it by reference to its boundaries, thus preventing any increase in land held by possession for the prescriptive period. Reference may be to walls, roads, the land of another person, or by measurement or a plan.

bowing — a form of agricultural contract whereby one party lets his herd to the other (the bower) for the bower to graze it on the former's land, while the bower retains the profits from eg dairy produce.

box — to lodge papers required in proceedings in the Court of Session for the clerk to place in the box for the appropriate judge or court officer (obsolete).

breach of contract — the failure by a party to a contract to implement any of its terms which are binding on him. If the breach is proved the injured party may claim damages, refuse to perform his obligations, rescind the contract or seek specific implement as appropriate in the circumstances.

breach of the peace — a common law offence of causing a public disturbance, such as fighting, shouting or swearing in a public place, or conduct causing or likely to cause annoyance, disturbance or disruption of the peace of the neighbourhood.

breath test — a preliminary test to obtain from a person's breath an indication whether the proportion of alcohol in his blood is likely to exceed the limit prescribed by road traffic legislation.

brevi manu — summarily; action taken to correct a wrong without seeking a remedy through the courts.

brevitatis causa — for the sake of brevity: a phrase frequently found in written pleadings to explain the incorporation by reference of the terms of some other document.

brieve —
  (1) a document once founding almost all civil actions in Scotland, but now in practice obsolete and superseded by the procedure on petition;
  (2) a warrant issued from Chancery to a judge, ordering an inquest by jury into certain specified matters.

brocard — a legal maxim derived from Roman law or ancient custom and accounted part of the common law.

bumping — the displacement of an employee by another who, because of reorganisation, is moved from one department to another.

burden — a limitation, restriction or incumbrance on the use, enjoyment, ownership etc of property. Burdens may be real or impose mere personal obligations.

burden of proof. *See* **onus of proof**.

burgage — an obsolete type of feudal tenure whereby property in royal burghs was held from the Crown.

burgh — a town brought into being or incorporated by royal charter or by or in accordance with statute. Since local government reorganisation in 1975 burghs no longer have any political or legal functions, having been absorbed by districts and islands areas. District courts have replaced the former burgh courts.

byelaw — subordinate legislation made eg by a local authority under power delegated by Parliament, and usually confirmed by some higher authority eg the Secretary of State.

C

caduciary — subject to lapse or escheat.

call — a demand for payment made by a company or its liquidators to those shareholders whose shares are not fully paid up.

calling — the publication of a summons in the Court of Session by posting, in a list on the walls of the court and in the printed rolls of court, the names of the parties and of the pursuer's legal representative. The time for entering appearance is determined by reference to the date of calling.

calling day — the day on which a summary cause (qv) summons in the sheriff court is first called before the sheriff clerk. The date is stated in the summons. Cf **return day**.

calling list. *See* **roll**.

camera — the chambers of a judge. Proceedings conducted there are heard *in camera*, ie in private.

Candlemas — a quarter day in Scotland (2 February).

capax — capable. Cf *incapax*.

capax doli — capable of or of an age to commit a crime.

caption — formerly a warrant for arrest in a civil process. As a 'process caption' it competently survives as a summary warrant to apprehend a solicitor to compel him to return to court a civil process which he has borrowed. As other normally effective remedies are available, it must be regarded now as a last resort!

case *or* **cause** — an action or proceeding in a civil court.

case law — judicial decisions as a source of law.

cash credit — a contract of loan under which the borrower may withdraw sums required up to a prescribed limit, and repays the sums periodically, paying interest only on the amount actually borrowed.

casual homicide — accidental killing where there is no fault on the part of the person causing the death.

casualty — a payment formerly due to a feudal superior or landlord on the occurrence of uncertain events. These payments are no longer exigible in respect of feus and are disallowed in respect of leases entered into after 1 September 1974.

casus amissionis — the occasion or circumstances of the loss, which must be shown when proving the tenor of a lost document.

casus improvisus — a case not provided for or not foreseen, frequently considered in the construction of rules, contracts and statutes.

casus omissus — a case omitted, where a situation has not been provided for within the existing law, especially in a statute.

catholic creditor — a creditor whose debt is secured over several subjects or the whole property of the debtor. He is bound to claim his debt according to equitable rules so as not to injure unnecessarily the claims of secondary creditors whose securities are postponed to his rights. Cf **secondary creditor**.

causa causans — the immediate cause; the effective or proximate cause of the harm occasioned where a duty has been breached.

causa cognita — a case known, heard and ready for judgment.

causa proxima, et non remota, spectatur — the near, and not the remote, cause is regarded. Eg a claimed loss must be a direct and not a remote consequence of a delict.

causa sine qua non — in the law of obligations, the cause but for which the harm would not have resulted. This is not necessarily the immediate cause.

cause. *See* **case**.

caution (pronounced 'kay-shun') —
   (1) in civil matters, security for a deed or a debt or for the administration of a trust estate;
   (2) in criminal practice, security for future good behaviour or as a condition of bail.

cautionary obligation — an obligation by way of caution (qv).

caveat — a formal notice to a court given by a party to proceedings to secure that no step affecting him will be taken in his absence or unless intimation is first given to him.

caveat emptor — let the buyer beware: a rule, basically of English law, much eroded by exceptions, both statutory and at common law.

certification — an assurance to a party to proceedings of the implied or specified consequences of his failure to obey the will of the writ or court order. Where the order invites appearance in court, the consequences of failure are usually that the case will proceed in that party's absence or, occasionally, a warrant for his arrest.

certiorate — to notify a fact formally.

certum est quod certum reddi potest — that is certain which can be made certain, such as a price, which may be established by reference to an authorised list or by measurement.

cess — an obsolete form of land tax.

cessante ratione legis cessat ipsa lex — when the reason for a law ceases, the law itself ceases to operate.

cessio bonorum — an obsolete action in which an insolvent debtor brought his creditors into court to surrender his assets to them in order to avoid imprisonment for debt.

chancellor — an obsolete term for the foreman of a jury.

Chancery Office — an office derived from that of the Lord Chancellor of Scotland, an appointment in abeyance since 1730. Certain Crown writs and commissions are issued from the Chancery Office by the Director of Chancery.

charge —
   (1) an order to obey a decree of court, including a written command served on a debtor to pay, on pain of poinding (qv);
   (2) a security over the property of a company;
   (3) a formal accusation of crime;
   (4) the direction given by a judge to a jury.

charter —
   (1) a deed comprising a grant of land by a feudal superior;
   (2) a royal grant of incorporation, with powers and privileges, to a public institution.

charterparty — a contract whereby a ship or part of a ship is hired for a fixed period or a specified voyage.

charters by progress — charters of confirmation or resignation formerly used to renew a right to land already held. They were so designated to distinguish them from the original charter (qv) creating the right.

chartulary — a mediaeval register containing copies of the owner's charters and other deeds.

child stealing. *See* *plagium*.

children's hearing — a hearing by a panel set up under the Social Work (Scotland) Act 1968 to deal with children who may be in need of compulsory measures of care.

chirographum apud debitorem repertum presumitur solutum — a bond or other document of debt, found in the possession of the debtor who granted it, is presumed to have been discharged.

circuit court — a court held by the judges of the High Court of Justiciary when sitting on circuit out of Edinburgh.

circumstantial evidence — indirect evidence of a fact when the fact cannot be established by direct evidence.

circumvention *or* **facility and circumvention** — conduct to persuade a weak minded or facile person to act against his interest. Any contract thus entered into would be thereby rendered voidable.

citation —
(1) the procedure whereby a defender is called to court to answer an action or a witness to give evidence;
(2) a reference in legal debate, argument or judgment to a supporting authority.

cite — to effect or make a citation (qv).

civil law —
(1) a synonym for 'private law' which is concerned with the rights and duties of persons and with settling disputes between them — the division between civil or private law and public law where the state or an organ of the state is involved is not altogether clear cut, but the distinction is usually convenient in practice;
(2) a synonym for Roman law.

civilian — a person learned in Roman law.

clare constat — it clearly appears: a precept (later a writ) granted by a superior in favour of the heir of a deceased vassal declaring that from the documents produced it clearly appears that the grantee is the heir. It was rendered unnecessary by the Succession (Scotland) Act 1964.

clause —
(1) a provision in a deed or instrument;
(2) a provision in a parliamentary Bill equivalent to a section in an Act of Parliament.

close season — a statutory period during which specified fish, animals or birds may not be taken or killed.

closed record — a document comprising the final written pleadings of the parties to a civil action. The court has 'closed' the record of the pleadings and leave is required for later amendments.

club — an association of people bound together by agreement for a particular purpose. Their rights and responsibilities are usually set forth in a constitution with rules. Where the assets and property of the club belong to the members, it is a members' club. Where they belong to an individual to whom the members pay a subscription, it is a proprietary club.

codicil — an addition to or alteration or revocation of a previous testamentary writing. The codicil is then construed with previous testamentary writings as a single document.

codifying Act — an Act which consolidates and collates all law from statutory and other sources on a particular subject into one piece of legislation. It is not to be confused with a consolidation Act (qv).

cognate — a person related to another on the mother's side, as distinct from an agnate, who is related on the father's side.

cognition — an obsolete legal process by which a person could be found insane by a jury and a curator appointed.

cognitionis causa tantum — have the amount of the debt ascertained; an action of declarator raised by the creditor of a deceased debtor for the purpose of constituting his debt.

collateral — a relative descended from the same ancestor but not in a direct line, eg a cousin.

collateral security — an additional security reinforcing the primary security for the performance of an obligation.

collatio inter haeredes — a bringing together among heirs. In the common law of succession, an heir-at-law who wished to participate in the legitim fund required to collate or bring in the heritable property to which he was heir as part of the fund. The principle was rendered obsolete by the Succession (Scotland) Act 1964.

collatio inter liberos — a bringing together among children. In the law of succession it still applies to the succession to the legitim fund of children of the deceased. Any advances made to a child by the deceased ancestor during his or her lifetime must be taken into account in calculating and distributing the legitim fund.

College of Justice — the Court of Session, established in 1532, comprising the Senators of the College of Justice (who are the judges of the Court of Session, addressed officially as Lords of Council and Session), advocates, Writers to the Signet, clerks of Session, keepers of the rolls and macers. The Law Society of Scotland and its members are not as such members of the College of Justice.

commissary — originally an ecclesiastical judge with jurisdiction in matters of personal status, eg legitimacy, marriage and succession. The Reformation did not abolish the functions of the Courts of the Officials in dioceses, but in 1563 a new Commissary Court was established in Edinburgh and each diocese. Until the 19th century the commissaries virtually monopolised jurisdiction in matters of status and succession. However, in 1832 the inferior commissaries were merged in the sheriff court, though they were not abolished until 1876, and the expression 'commissary' survives in the description of executing matters as 'commissary business'.

commission — the authorisation by the court granted in the course of an action to a qualified person to take evidence from a witness who cannot attend court or, with diligence, to recover documents.

Commissioner for Local Administration in Scotland — the local government ombudsman. On a complaint by a member of the public who may have suffered an injustice through maladministration, the commissioner has power to investigate the acts and actions of certain authorities and may make recommendations and state his conclusions to the appropriate authorities or government departments. See the Local Government (Scotland) Act 1975, s 23.

Commissioner of Teinds — a judge of the Court of Session appointed to sit in the Court of Teinds, which is in effect a function of the Court of Session. Since the business of the Court of Teinds is now almost entirely formal and unopposed, usually a Lord Ordinary sits as a Lord Commissioner of Teinds, with the Teind Clerk, and deals with its ministerial and judicial functions. *See* **teind.**

commissioners in a sequestration — up to five persons who may be appointed by creditors from their own number or their mandatories following a sequestration under the Bankruptcy (Scotland) Act 1985 to supervise the permanent trustee in bankruptcy.

committal — the ordering of a person charged under a petition of the procurator fiscal to be detained in custody pending further inquiry or, when 'fully committed', until liberated in due course of law.

commixtion — the mixing of solid (as contrasted with liquid) moveables belonging to different owners, thus affecting their property rights. The consequences vary depending upon whether the mixture is or is not capable of subsequent separation or has been made as a result of consent, accident or fault.

commodatum — the gratuitous loan of an article which the borrower must return in the same form and state as when borrowed.

common agent — a solicitor employed to conduct a cause in which several parties have a common interest, eg ranking and sale or multiplepoinding.

common calamity — a fatal event in which two or more persons die with no indication of which predeceased. If they were husband and wife, neither is presumed to have survived the other; otherwise, generally the older is presumed to have predeceased the younger. See the Succession (Scotland) Act 1964, s 31.

common debtor — where the effects of a debtor have been arrested and several creditors claim a share of them, the debtor, as being debtor to all, is designated as the common debtor in related proceedings.

common good — property of a district or islands council derived other than from rates or central government grants. Former royal burghs received grants of land, taxes, tolls etc from the Crown to sustain the dignity of the burgh.

common interest — an interest less than a right of property which justifies the party exercising it in having some control in the use of the property; eg, in the case of a mutual wall between two houses, a party with common interest may resist any injurious alteration.

common law — law which does not stem from a statute. It includes law as laid down in judicial decisions and in authoritative writings, and is mainly derived from Roman, canon and feudal law and custom.

common property — property, either immoveable or moveable, belonging to two or more owners *pro indiviso*, ie in an undivided manner with no separation of shares. Each co-owner may sell his undivided share. In matters of administration, except in the case of necessary operations, the wishes of an owner objecting to a course of action prevail. However, any owner may compel division of the property. *See also **pro indiviso**.*

commonty — a right neither of common property nor of common interest but of joint perpetual use of land by adjoining commoners eg for pasturing. The Division of Commonties Act 1695 (c 38) provides for division, and commonty is now virtually obsolete.

communings — negotiations which do or may result in a contract, usually called 'prior communings'.

community charge — a *per capita* charge imposed by a local authority on persons resident in its area for the purpose of providing funds to enable the authority to discharge its statutory functions so far as the cost thereof is not otherwise met or provided for. From 1 April 1989 to 31 March 1993 community charges were payable in Scotland.

community council — an elected body established by a scheme made by an islands or district council to ascertain, co-ordinate and express the views of the community which it represents and to take such action in the interests of the community as appears to it to be expedient and practicable.

community service order — an order of a criminal court under the Community Service by Offenders (Scotland) Act 1978, requiring an offender to do useful work within the community instead of being fined or imprisoned.

commute — to change into another form, eg when feudal casualties were converted into increased annual feuduty, or cancelled by a lump sum payment.

compear — to appear as a party in court, in person or by counsel or agent.

compensatio injuriarum — compensation of wrongs; an obsolete plea, formerly found in actions of defamation, to set off claims for mutual injuries against each other.

compensation — the extinction of mutual similar claims by setting one off against the other. There must be *concursus debiti et crediti* (qv).

compensation order — an order for the payment of compensation to an injured party by a person convicted of an offence which has caused injury, loss or damage. See the Criminal Justice (Scotland) Act 1980, Pt IV (ss 58–67).

competence — the authority of a court to entertain a particular type of case or form of procedure.

competency — the admissibility of evidence or of a particular witness are matters of competency.

competent and omitted — describes a preliminary plea against an argument which could have been but was not advanced in an earlier litigation.

complaint — a document instituting summary criminal proceedings in a sheriff or district court, setting out the offence charged.

composition — an arrangement between a debtor and his creditors whereby the debtor's debts are discharged in exchange for agreed partial payment. Composition may take the form of an extra-judicial contract or, after sequestration, proceed under the Bankruptcy (Scotland) Act 1985, Sch 4.

conclude — to claim a remedy in a summons in civil procedure in the Court of Session. *See* **conclusion.**

conclusion — the statement in a summons in civil proceedings in the Court of Session of the precise remedy claimed. *See also* **crave.**

concourse — the concurrence of the public prosecutor in a private prosecution.

concursus debiti et crediti — concourse or concurrence of debt and credit: a prerequisite of a plea of compensation, which can be founded only where each party is debtor and creditor, each in his own right, at the same time. *See* **compensation.**

condescendence — statement(s) of fact by the pursuer in civil pleadings.

condictio — a personal action, contrasted with *vindicatio,* a real action.

condictio causa data causa non secuta — claim that the consideration has failed of its purpose: the claim that, payment or performance having been given, and the counterpart consideration having failed, as with prepayments, the money paid or the value of the performance be restored under the principles of unjustified enrichment.

condictio indebiti — claim that payment was not due: an action for the repayment of money paid in the erronious belief that a debt was due.

conditio si institutus sine liberis decesserit — the condition if the beneficiary dies childless: an implied condition in a will that where a bequest is made to a group of the testator's family, and a named beneficiary in that group dies before the testator, the issue of that beneficiary takes the beneficiary's share in preference to other legatees and heirs.

conditio si testator sine liberis decesserit — the condition if the testator dies childless: a rebuttable presumption applicable where a parent who makes a will without provision for a child then has a child and dies without altering it. The law may presume that the will has been revoked because the deceased testator would have wished to make provision for the child.

condition — a clause in a contract or disposition qualifying an obligation therein contained. Conditions may be suspensive or precedent, indicating postponement of the obligation until the condition is fulfilled, or resolutive, indicating that the obligation ceases upon fulfilment of the condition.

confer — compare (abbreviated 'cf').

confirmation — power judicially conferred on the executor of a deceased person's estate to administer the estate. By confirmation an executor gains title to the property and assets of the deceased.

conform (adj) — in conformity. A 'decree conform' is a judgment by one court giving effect to the judgment of another, eg so as to enable diligence to be done.

confusio —
  (1) the commingling of liquids: *see* **commixtion**;
  (2) a form of accession by which an obligation may be extinguished, eg where a debtor acquires the rights of his creditor, or where the proprietor of a servient tenement becomes proprietor of the dominant tenement.

conjoin — to join two causes into one. The court has a discretion to conjoin causes which are related to the same subject matter, raise the same question or are otherwise so connected that it is expedient that they be tried together and disposed of in the same manner. On conjunction the two causes become one.

conjoined arrestment order — an order by way of diligence against the earnings of a debtor in the hands of his employer to enforce the payment of two or more debts owed to different creditors against the same earnings.

conjunct — rights taken by two or more persons jointly. Thus a grant to two unrelated persons 'in conjunct fee and liferent and their heirs' makes them equal fiars during the joint lives, the survivor taking the liferent of the whole, and on his death the fee divides equally between the heirs of both.

conjunct and several obligation — an obligation (also called a 'joint and several obligation') in which each obligant is individually bound, irrespective of the duties of co-obligants, to render complete performance if called upon to do so.

conjunct or confident persons — persons closely related by blood or affinity or being in a situation of 'intimate and confidential intercourse'. Alienations to conjunct or confident persons without due cause by a person verging on insolvency were to be annulled under the Bankruptcy Act 1621. The Bankruptcy (Scotland) Act 1985 repeals the earlier statute and now uses the term 'associate' (qv) (s 74).

conjunct probation or proof — the process of disproving by evidence an opponent's averments while also proving one's own averments.

conjunction. *See* **conjoin**.

consanguinean — describes relations descended from the same father, but not from the same mother, eg half sisters. Cf **uterine**.

consensus in idem — consent as to the same essentials; agreement as to those matters in a contract which are essential to make the contract binding. There is no consent if eg one party consents to hire and the other consents to sale.

consignation — the deposit with the clerk of court or a third party, under the authority of the court, of money or a moveable in dispute.

consistorial action — proceedings derived from the jurisdiction formerly exercised by the Commissary Courts in matters of marital status. It included actions of divorce, of separation, of declarator of marriage, of legitimacy, of freedom and putting to silence, of adherence and of aliment between husband and wife. For certain purposes it remains an important term of art. The sheriff court has had concurrent jurisdiction with the Court of Session in actions of separation since 1907 and in divorce since 1984.

consolidation — the bringing together in the same person of the two estates in land of superiority (*dominium directum*) and of vassalage (*dominium utile*) which have hitherto been separately vested in that person.

consolidation Act — an Act which incorporates in one Act and supersedes some or all of the provisions of a number of earlier Acts relating to the same subject matter.

constitute — to establish (usually through a judgment) the fact that a debt exists. This may be necessary after the debtor or original creditor has died.

constructive — having legal effect, even though the thing described may not exist as a fact, eg constructive knowledge or constructive total loss.

consuetudo pro lege servatur — custom is observed as law. All Scots law, except legislation, is ultimately customary or common law.

consultation —
(1) a power of the judges of a Division of the Inner House of the Court of Session, in cases of importance or difficulty or where the judges are equally divided, to state questions of law for the opinion of the other judges of the court;
(2) a meeting between counsel and solicitor, with or without the client, to discuss a case.

contemporanea expositio — contemporaneous construction: a rule that the meaning or construction of old Acts of Parliament, deeds and contracts which they had or were given at the time they were made should, in case of doubt, prevail.

contempt of court — insulting, disorderly or disobedient behaviour towards a court, or acts calculated to obstruct the course of justice or flouting the court's authority. Courts have summary power to punish for contempt, subject to a right of appeal.

contingency — a situation which warrants a court remitting an action *ob contingentiam* to another court dealing with another action. It arises eg where in the two actions the same parties are in dispute about the same matter, or where the second action arises directly out of the first, or where, though the parties are different, the subject matter is the same and the decision in one will decide the matter as regards the whole world. On remission the actions remain distinct, but one may be sisted to await the result of the other. Cf **conjoin.**

continue — to defer or adjourn proceedings to a later date.

contra bonos mores — against decent moral standards. Thus contracts or obligations for an immoral consideration are unenforceable.

contra proferentem — against the person putting it forward. Thus an ambiguous term in a contract may be construed against the person who inserted it.

contributory negligence — some careless or blameworthy act or omission by the pursuer which contributed, with the defender's fault or negligence, to the pursuer's loss or injury. Since 1945 the court may reduce an award of damages in proportion to the pursuer's share of responsibility for what happened.

contumacy — stubborn or wilful refusal to obey a court order, whence contumacious.

conventional obligation — an obligation arising from an agreement or contract, as distinct from one created by the general law, as in the case of delict or unjust enrichment.

convicium — a delict involving the communication of true or false material designed to hold a person up to hatred, ridicule or contempt.

corporeal moveables — physical objects which are capable of being moved, as distinct from heritable property.

corpus delicti — the substance or body of facts constituting a crime or offence charged.

corroboration — evidence which confirms other evidence of fact. Corroboration was normally required for 'full proof' in Scots law but is no longer essential in civil proceedings: see the Civil Evidence (Scotland) Act 1988, s 1. Subject to certain exceptions, a crucial or primary fact cannot be proved by the testimony of one witness alone. There had to be either the direct testimony of two witnesses or two or more evidential facts each spoken to by one or more witnesses from which a crucial fact could be inferred. Documentary or real evidence may provide corroboration.

counsel — an advocate; a member of the Faculty of Advocates.

count reckoning and payment — an action to require the defender to render an account of his dealings or intromissions with property which does not belong to him but which has been entrusted to him, and to pay to the person entitled any balance which may be found to be due on the account.

counter action — an action raised by the defender to another action in order to clarify his position. The defender is not bound to await the pleasure of the pursuer as to the prosecution of the first action; hence his right to raise a counter action, although there must be a slight difference between the issues or a plea of *lis alibi pendens* will be sustained. *See also,* in the context of divorce, **cross action.**

counterclaim — a claim by a defender which may competently be made and dealt with in the principal action even though it could have formed the basis of independent proceedings initiated by the defender.

Court of Criminal Appeal — a court, of which three Lords Commissioners of Justiciary form a quorum, constituted to hear appeals against conviction and sentence by persons convicted on indictment. No further appeal is competent. Cf **High Court of Justiciary.**

Court of Exchequer — a court created after the Union of 1707 to determine revenue matters. It was merged with the Court of Session in 1856, although revenue matters are still heard as Exchequer causes.

Court of Session — the supreme civil court in Scotland. The judges of the court's Outer House, sitting alone, determine cases at first instance. The two Divisions (qv) of the Inner House have primarily an appellate jurisdication. In certain conditions the decisions of the Inner House are appealable to the House of Lords.

court of summary jurisdiction — a court where criminal cases are dealt with by a judge sitting alone without a jury. The district court has summary jurisdiction only, but the sheriff court exercises both summary and solemn jurisdiction.

Court of Teinds. *See* **Commissioner of Teinds.**

courtesy — the liferent in the heritage of a deceased wife, conferred on a widower (obsolete since 1964).

court-martial — a court appointed to hear charges of breach of service discipline by members of HM forces or civilian employees of the forces. The court usually comprises a number of officers advised by a judge advocate (qv).

Courts-Martial Appeal Court — a United Kingdom court constituted to hear appeals against conviction by court-martial.

crave —
  (1) the statement in an initial writ in a sheriff court action of the precise remedy sought (cf **conclusion**);
  (2) to ask a court for something.

creditor — a person to whom a debtor is obliged. In Scots law the term is not restricted to monetary obligations. A secured creditor is one to whom the debtor has granted security for the sum due. Some creditors may have preferential claims (eg in sequestrations and in executries).

crime. *See* **offence.**

crimen falsi — the crime of falsehood: any crime known to the law consisting in falsehood, eg forgery, perjury and fraud.

croft — an agricultural holding situated in one of the crofting counties (qv). Such holdings have been regulated exclusively by statute. A crofter who has not purchased the land which forms his croft does not own the croft land or croft house but is a tenant of both and has security of tenure as tenant.

crofting counties — the area to which the statutes relating to crofting apply, comprising the seven former counties of Argyll, Caithness, Inverness, Orkney, Ross and Cromarty, Sutherland and Shetland.

cross action — an action for divorce raised by a party to a marriage who is being sued by the other for divorce.

cross-examination — the examination of a witness by the other party or parties after examination-in-chief. Leading questions are allowed in cross-examination, but not in examination-in-chief. The questions must be relevant to the issues in dispute, but considerable latitude is allowed.

Crown —
(1) the sovereign;
(2) in relation to rights, interests, privileges, criminal prosecutions etc, Her Majesty's government, analogous to the term 'the state', 'the people' or 'the Commonwealth' in other jurisdictions. Probably the concept of 'the Crown' has discouraged constitutional analysis of the concept of 'the state'.

Crown Agent — the most senior official on the staff of the Crown Office (qv). The Crown Agent, whose primary concern is with the criminal process, also acts as the government solicitor if the Crown Office or Lord Advocate's Department become involved in a civil action.

Crown Office — a department under the Lord Advocate responsible for the public prosecution of crime within Scotland. Crown counsel in the High Court of Justiciary are assisted by Crown Office officials, who also administer the procurator fiscal service. Some functions of the Queen's and Lord Treasurer's Remembrancer have been transferred to the Crown Office.

cujus est solum, ejus est usque ad coelum — whoever owns the land owns everything above it, eg buildings and fruits.

culpa — fault. Derived from the Lex Aquilia of Roman law as developed by the civilians, in its broadest sense *culpa* implies fault generally, whether intentional or negligent. In modern practice *culpa* in the narrower sense of negligence is more familiar, ie a breach of a legal duty to take reasonable care in the particular circumstances, but the comprehensive concept of *culpa* distinguishes Scots delict from English tort.

culpa lata dolo aequiparatur — gross negligence is treated as fraud, ie as if it were intentional.

culpable homicide — comprises all aspects of homicide which are neither casual nor justifiable, on the one hand, nor murderous on the other. Death which results from assault or negligent criminal acts are prosecuted as culpable homicide. The crime also includes cases where there has been no intent to kill but there are circumstances of diminished responsibility or provocation. Cf manslaughter in English law.

cum decimis inclusis — including teinds. If land is feued *cum decimis inclusis,* the titular (ie the person entitled to teinds) cannot claim payment.

cum nota — with a mark; describes evidence admitted with some reservation, eg the evidence of an accomplice.

curator. *See* **curatory.**

curator ad litem — a curator appointed by the court to act for a person under disability (eg by reason of youth or mental disorder) whose interests have to be safeguarded in legal proceedings.

curator bonis — a curator appointed to act generally for a person incapable through illness or absence of administering his own affairs.

curatory — the office of an administrator who acts for or consents to the legal actings of an *incapax* (ie a person legally incapable of acting on his own account). Thus a curator supplements the capacity of minors by consenting to their acts.

current maintenance arrestment — a form of diligence against the earnings of a debtor in the hands of his employer to enforce the payment of current maintenance.

custom —
  (1) judicial custom or *usus fori,* the method by which the judges developed the
      common law through judicial decisions;
  (2) a generally accepted unwritten rule which, if embodied in the common law by
      reason of its acceptance by the community, need not be proved;
  (3) such a rule, not recognised by the law, but which may, if reasonable, be binding on
      the parties to a contract if they or their community or trade accept it, although it
      must be proved by evidence.

cy-près **scheme** — a 'so-near' scheme approved by the Court of Session, in the exercise
  of its *nobile officium,* under which, where literal effect cannot be given to the intention
  of the donor or testator under a charitable gift or bequest, or where it would be
  unreasonable or in excess of what the law permits to do so, or where the circumstances
  have changed, the court allows the funds to be applied as nearly as possible or
  practicable to the apparent intended purpose.

d

damages — a sum of money claimed as compensation for loss, injury or damage
  resulting from an act or omission of the defender which is in breach of a duty owed,
  either as a result of voluntary obligation or by force of law. The amount of damages
  awarded is intended to put the person entitled thereto as nearly as may be in the same
  position as he was before the harm occurred.

damnum — loss or damage, injury or harm.

damnum absque (or sine) injuria — loss or damage suffered, but not as the result of a legal
  wrong, and therefore not reparable.

damnum fatale — loss caused by an unusual accident, such as exceptional storm or other
  natural calamity which could not reasonably have been foreseen, and consequently the
  resulting loss could not have been prevented. It is sometimes called an Act of God (its
  equivalent in English law).

damnum injuria datum — loss caused by a legal wrong or fault: the basis of liability in
  delict. If there is no legal wrong (eg if there is statutory authority for the act causing the
  loss) there may be no liability.

de die in diem — from day to day; daily.

de facto — in fact; existing as an objective fact, albeit not necessarily based on any rule of
  law. Thus the *de facto* situation is the actual or factual situation. Cf *de jure.*

de fideli administratione officii — of the faithful administration of the office: the oath
  taken by a person appointed to perform some public office or duty, undertaking to
  carry it out faithfully.

de jure — as a matter of law or in point of law. Cf *de facto.*

de liquido in liquidum — of a liquid claim against a liquid claim; compensation or set-off.

de minimis non curat lex — the law does not concern itself with trifles. Thus the courts
  will not provide an equitable remedy for a trivial complaint. The maxim is not usually
  found in criminal procedure.

de minimis non curat praetor — the judge does not concern himself with trifles. A less
  familiar but more strictly accurate version of *de minimis non curat lex* (qv).

de momento in momentum — from moment to moment. Thus prescription runs *de
  momento in momentum,* ie to the very last minute.

de novo — anew, afresh; starting again from the beginning.

de plano — immediately; summarily, without further formality.

de presenti — now, at the present time.

de recenti — recent. Thus a *de recenti* statement made by a victim soon after the alleged
  commission of eg a sexual offence may reinforce the victim's evidence by enhancing its

credibility, but does not provide corroboration. Possession *de recenti* of stolen goods may create the presumption that the possessor is the thief.

dead's part — that part of the moveable estate of a deceased person which, after the legal rights of any surviving spouse, children or their issue have been deducted, the deceased may dispose of by will in any way he wishes.

Dean of Faculty — the elected leader of the Faculty of Advocates (qv), or of a local Faculty or society of solicitors.

Dean of Guild — formerly the head of the Guild, Brethren or Merchant Company in certain burghs, with jurisdiction in mercantile and maritime causes, and latterly elected by a town council to preside over a Dean of Guild Court (qv).

Dean of Guild Court — a court constituted, until the reorganisation of local government in 1975, by the Dean of Guild, sitting alone or with others, with jurisdiction in respect of the construction of buildings throughout certain burghs. From 1959, in other burghs and in the landward area of counties, this jurisdiction was exercised by a buildings authority consisting of not less than three councillors.

debitum fundi or debitum reale — a real debt, lien or obligation over land which attaches to the land itself.

debitum in presenti solvendum in futuro — a debt now due but not payable until a future date, eg a legacy payable out of an estate on the expiry of a liferent.

debitum reale. See debitum fundi.

debt — money legally owed.

decern — to give a final and extractable decree or judgment. Actual use of this formal expression is no longer necessary to warrant the issue of extract.

decimae — tenth parts or teinds. *See also* **cum decimis inclusis.**

declaration — a formal statement before a sheriff made by an accused person at or after his first appearance in court.

declarator — a declaration by the court of a person's rights, made in an action for declarator. The declarator does not itself actually enforce the rights. There has to be a practical rather than a theoretical purpose to the action.

declinature — the rule that a judge must decline to hear a cause in which he has an interest, whether because of relationship to the parties (Declinature Act 1681) or because of pecuniary interest. The rule extends to the refusal of other appointments, eg as trustee.

decree (the first syllable is stressed) — the final judgment of a court or arbiter in civil proceedings. A decree may order the defender to pay, perform or abstain from performing some act, or may exonerate him if the pursuer has failed to establish his claim. *See also* **extract decree.**

decree arbitral — the final judgment of an arbiter.

decree conform — a decree authorising the enforcement of an order or decree of some other court or body.

decree dative — a judgment appointing a person to be an executor.

deed — a formal document, executed and authenticated in accordance with prescribed formalities and incorporating the terms of an agreement, contract or obligation.

deed of arrangement — a contract between competing claimants, such as creditors or beneficiaries, in which the distribution of property is agreed.

deeming — a legal fiction often adopted in legislation whereby a thing or situation is stated to be as stated, whether or not this corresponds to fact or reality. Thus something can be deemed to be something else.

defences — a statement lodged by the defender in a civil action, setting out in numbered paragraphs the facts and legal propositions constituting his answers to the pursuer's claim.

defender — the party against whom a civil action has been raised.

defer sentence — to adjourn a criminal case after a person has been convicted or found to have committed an offence for his good behaviour or to enable inquiries to be made to help the court to determine sentence or final disposal.

deforcement — the crime of resisting or obstructing officers of the law who are enforcing a decree or judicial warrant.

del credere — describes an agreement with an agent whereby, for additional remuneration, the agent guarantees to his principal the performance by a third person of a contract into which the principal has entered.

delectus personae — the choice of a specific person because of personal considerations. A person so chosen may not delegate or assign any duty imposed on him.

delegation — the substitution, with the creditor's consent, of a new debtor for the old, thus extinguishing the liability of the old debtor.

delegatus non potest delegare — a representative cannot devolve the powers entrusted to him by another.

delict — a civil wrong created by the deliberate or negligent breach of a legal duty, from which a liability to compensate consequential loss and injury may arise.

deliverance — an interlocutor or court order commonly used in sequestration proceedings.

delivery —
(1) the transfer of possession of a corporeal moveable from one person to another;
(2) the acknowledgment by a person, by words or conduct, of his intention to be bound by a deed as a prerequisite for its effectiveness, usually signified by actual delivery but recording in the appropriate register may be equally effective.

denuding — the divesting by a trustee of the trust estate on his demitting office.

deponent — a witness who makes a deposition (qv).

deportation order — an order requiring an alien to leave the United Kingdom and prohibiting his re-entry.

deposit; deposition —
(1) strictly, a gratuitous contract under which corporeal moveable property is entrusted by the depositor to the depository for safe custody, the contract being for the sole benefit of the depositor (the term is now extended to include custody for reward);
(2) a sum deposited as a pledge;
(3) the initial payment under a hire purchase agreement;
(4) a payment made to the credit of a bank account.

deposition — a statement made by a witness (a deponent) on oath and recorded in writing.

dereliction — definitive abandonment of property.

desert the diet — to abandon a criminal charge, either *simpliciter* (irrevocably) or *pro loco et tempore* (for this place and time). In the latter case a new charge may be brought.

design — to set out a person's designation (qv).

designation — a person's style, title, name, description, address, marital status etc.

destination — a direction, usually in a disposition or will, prescribing the order of succession to moveable and heritable property.

destination over — a clause providing that if a designated beneficiary fails to take a gift, it is to pass to another.

detention — a punishment whereby young persons under the age of twenty-one are kept or detained in custody for a fixed period of time.

devil — an aspirant for admission to the Faculty of Advocates (qv) who trains as an assistant to an established advocate.

dictum — a statement made by a judge in the course of a judgment.

dies cedit — *dies cedit* imports that an obligation has come into existence but is not yet prestable, and *dies venit* imports that the time for its enforcement has arrived.

dies dominicus non est juridicus — Sunday is not a 'lawful' day, in the sense that it is not a day recognised as appropriate for most judicial or legal proceedings.

dies incertus pro conditione habetur — an uncertain day is treated as a condition. Thus a promise of payment on the occasion of one's marriage is a conditional obligation which comes into effect only on the marriage.

dies interpellat pro homine — the day interrupts the man: the arrival of the stipulated day of performance of an obligation is enough, and no further action by the creditor is required. Failure to perform will attract the appropriate penalties, eg interest on any sum due.

dies non — a day (eg a Sunday or public holiday) when judicial proceedings are not conducted.

dies venit. *See* **dies cedit**.

diet — a date fixed by a court for the hearing of a case.

dilatory defence — a defence in civil proceedings that does not go to the merits of the case and is designed to delay it.

diligence —
  (1) the methods of enforcing unpaid debts due under decrees of the Scottish courts: enforcement of judgments;
  (2) in litigation, the process of enforcing the recovery of evidence from an opponent or third person.

diminished responsibility — a state of mental instability or weakness, falling short of insanity, which, if established, may justify reducing the quality of the crime of murder to culpable homicide or otherwise mitigate the guilt of the accused.

dispone — to convey land. Formerly the use of the word in a deed was indispensible for the validity of a disposition of land.

discharge —
  (1) the formal release of a debtor from an obligation, sometimes without full payment or performance;
  (2) the release of a bankrupt from the disabilities of sequestration;
  (3) a receipt.

discuss — to use diligence against the principal debtor before using it against a cautioner. *See also* **beneficium ordinis**.

disposition — a formal deed transferring heritable or moveable property.

dispositive clause — the clause in a disposition by which the property is transferred.

dissent — to disagree with the majority opinion. Thus a dissenting judgment disagrees with the opinions of the majority of the bench.

district — a sub-division of a region (qv) for local government purposes. The local authority is the district council.

district court — a court established in each district or islands area by the District Courts (Scotland) Act 1975 with a jurisdiction, concerned with less serious criminal offences, exercised by justices of the peace (who need not be legally qualified) or legally-qualified stipendiary magistrates. On the introduction of district courts the former justice of the peace courts, quarter sessions, burgh courts and the Court of the Bailie of the River and Firth of Clyde were abolished.

Division — a component of the Inner House of the Court of Session. The First Division is presided over by the Lord President and the second Division by the Lord Justice-Clerk. There is occasionally an Extra Division.

division — an action by a *pro indiviso* proprietor for the division of property held in common with other proprietors.

divorce — judicial dissolution of marriage.

divot. *See* **feal and divot**.

dock — an enclosure in a courtroom where the accused person sits during a criminal trial.

docket *or* **docquet** —
  (1) an authenticating indorsement on a deed or other document;
  (2) in obsolete conveyancing practice, a holograph attestation appended to a notarial instrument.

document of debt — a document constituting evidence of a legal transaction or itself creating indebtedness, eg a bill of exchange.

document of title — a document which provides evidence of a legal entitlement to property.

dole. *See* **malus animus**.

dolus — fraud; 'every trick, falsehood or device employed for the purpose of circumventing, cheating or deceiving another' (Dig 4, 3, 1, 2).

domicile — the place where a person is considered by law to have his permanent home.

dominant tenement — land the ownership of which includes a servitude over adjoining land, called the 'servient tenement'.

dominium directum — the residual but radical rights in land enjoyed by the superior who has granted the effective ownership (the *dominium utile*) to a vassal.

dominium utile — the effective right of ownership of land enjoyed by a vassal, generally regarded as full ownership subject to certain rights (the *dominium directum*) of the superior through the superior's feudal title.

dominus litis — the master of the litigation: the effective party to legal proceedings which may be carried on in the name of another. The *dominus litis* may be ordered to pay the expenses involved.

domitae naturae — of a tamed nature, as of tamed or domestic animals as distinguished from animals *ferae naturae* (qv).

donatio inter virum et uxorem — a gift between husband and wife.

donation *inter vivos* — a gift made by one person to another whilst both parties are alive, contrasted with donation *mortis causa* (qv).

donation *mortis causa* — a gift made in contemplation of death and effective only on the donor's death. A gift may be transferred prior to the donor's death, but if the donee predeceases the donor the gift reverts to the donor.

donatory — a person to whom the Crown gives property which has fallen to the Crown by forfeiture or failure of succession.

doom — judgment; sentence.

double distress — two or more competing claims to a fund or to property on separate and hostile grounds, a prerequisite to an action of multiplepoinding.

double jeopardy — prosecution twice for what, in substance, is the same crime or offence.

double ranking — claiming twice against the same estate. No debt may be ranked twice upon a sequestrated estate. Thus if the principal and the cautioner are both bankrupt, a creditor may rank in each estate but the cautioner may not then rank in the principal's estate.

dubitante — doubting; used of a judge expressing doubt or reservations in his judgment.

durante bene placito — during good pleasure, as of an office or appointment the holder of which may be dismissed at the pleasure of the person appointing him. Contrast with an appointment *ad vitam aut culpam* (qv).

duress — strictly a term of English law equivalent to force and fear, *vi ac metus*, or coercion in Scots law. It may be relevant as a ground for annulling obligations in the context of civil law or as a mitigating factor in criminal law.

duty solicitor — a solicitor available under the legal aid scheme at the sheriff court of all areas on all court days, whose services are available to persons in custody on charges of murder or culpable homicide, or appearing before the sheriff on peitition on solemn procedure, or in custody on their first appearance before the sheriff on summary complaint.

dying declaration — a statement made on his deathbed by a witness which, after his death, may be admissible evidence in a criminal trial.

dying deposition — a dying declaration made on oath.

e

eadem persona cum defuncto — the same person as the deceased. An executor is deemed to stand in the shoes of the deceased and is liable for the debts of the deceased up to the extent of the assets of the deceased.

earnings arrestment — a form of diligence against the earnings of a debtor in the hands of his employer to enforce the payment of a debt.

eavesdrop *or* **stillicide** — a servitude imposing on a servient tenement the burden of receiving rainwater droppings from the eaves of the dominant tenement.

edict *nautae, caupones, stabularii* — the praetorian edict whereby shipmasters, innkeepers and stable keepers were strictly liable, without proof of fault, for the loss of or damage to travellers' property. It was adopted as a principle of Scots law.

edictal citation — the citation of a person subject to the court's jurisdiction but who is furth of Scotland or whose whereabouts are unknown, by delivery to the Keeper of Edictal Citations of a copy of the summons, which is entered in a register.

Edinburgh Gazette — the official periodical government newspaper in Scotland. Numerous statutes require notice of certain events or steps taken in proceedings to be advertised in it. There are also a London Gazette and a Belfast Gazette.

effeiring to — relating to; pertaining to; often applied to ancillary rights transferred along with heritable property.

eik (pronounced 'eek') — an extension of the confirmation of an executor to include property not included in the original inventory.

ejection —
(1) an action to remove or eject a person who is in possession of heritable property without title (cf **removing**);
(2) the warrant following upon a decree of removing against a tenant on termination of the lease or on irritancy;
(3) the unlawful removal of a person from possession of heritable property.

ejusdem generis — of the same kind or nature: a rule of interpretation, especially of statutes or deeds, whereby where particular classes are specified by name, followed by general words, the meaning of the general words is limited by reference to the particular classes and the general words are taken to apply only to things of the same kind or nature as the particular classes.

elide — to oust, annul or exclude.

embezzle — to use money or property fraudulently to one's own advantage after lawfully receiving it for another purpose.

employer and employee — a legal relationship in which one person engages another to perform work or provide services under his direction or control.

Employment Appeal Tribunal — an appellate court comprising, in Scotland, a Court of Session judge and two lay members representing employers and employees, which considers appeals on questions of law from decisions of industrial tribunals (qv).

encumbrance — a burden, especially a debt or obligation secured over land.

endorse. *See* **indorse**.

engross — to produce a fair copy of a deed or other legal instrument in its final form, ready for signature or execution.

enorm lesion — serious injury to the estate of a minor child which may entitle him to the reduction, within four years of his majority, of a contract which caused it.

enrol the cause — to lodge a cause or case or some related document in court to enable it to be called, usually on a particular date.

entail, tailzie *or* **tailye** — a form of disposition of heritable property on a specified line of successive heirs to keep the property in the family. It often includes special provisions regarding forfeiture, alienation and borrowing. New entails have been prohibited since 1914.

enterprise zone — a designated part of the area of a local authority in which investment in new commercial enterprises is stimulated eg by the simplification of planning procedures.

entry — the act of taking possession of land as of right, eg by a purchaser. Title is completed by recording in the General Register of Sasines or the Land Register of Scotland.

enumeratio unius est exclusio alterius. See *expressio unius est exclusio alterius.*

eo die — that day; the same day.

eo nomine — in that name or character.

equipollent — an equivalent. Thus, if a statute or an agreement prescribes a particular form of procedure, equipollents are inadmissible.

error — mistaken belief. Error as to an essential fact may render a contract void according to one influential interpretation, or voidable. Error as to law is generally irrelevant.

error calculi — a mistake in calculation.

errore lapsus — a mistake through error.

escheat — forfeiture or confiscation: an obsolete penalty affecting a person's estate.

estate — all the property that a person owns, both heritable and moveable. 'Landed estate' is limited to heritable property.

esto — if it be so; a word frequently found in written pleadings to announce an assumption, which is not otherwise admitted, in order to state an alternative or consequential case, eg '*Esto* the pursuer slipped and fell as he avers, which is denied, he negligently failed to keep a good lookout.'

et sequentes paginae — and following pages (abbreviated '*et seq*').

evidents — writs and deeds proving a title to land (obsolete).

ex adverso — opposite to; describing the position of land or buildings.

ex contractu — arising from a contract. The phrase can refer to both a right and an obligation under a contract.

ex deliberatione Dominorum Concilii — after consideration by the Lords of Council: a term of art indicating that a writ can pass the Signet (qv) in the Court of Session, thus enabling it to be issued. Formerly all writs required to be read, considered and approved by the Lord Ordinary on the Bills before they could pass the Signet.

ex delicto — arising from a delict.

ex dolo non oritur actio — a right of action does not arise out of fraud. Thus a guilty party may not enforce a fraudulent obligation or contract.

ex facie — on the face of it. Generally something *ex facie* correct is presumed to be so until the contrary is established.

ex facie **absolute disposition** — an apparently absolute disposition of property which was truly granted by the owner as security for a loan and was accompanied by a back letter or explanatory letter making it clear that the disponee (often a building society) did not in fact own the property absolutely but only by way of security. The system was superseded by the standard security in 1970.

ex gratia — gratuitous, done without recognising any legal obligation to do whatever was done. Thus an *ex gratia* payment may be made to settle a claim without any admission as to liability.

ex hypothesi — from the hypothesis; put forward as a theory.

ex lege — according to law. Thus interest on money lent may be due to the creditor *ex lege* from the date of repayment even if there was no specific agreement between the parties as to interest.

ex nobile officium — on account of or by virtue of the *nobile officium* (qv).

ex nudo pacto non oritur actio — no right of action arises from a bare promise or engagement. A promise or bargain without a consideration is an unenforceable obligation: a principle of civil law adopted in England, but not in Scotland where gratuitous obligations are enforceable.

ex officio — by virtue of holding a particular appointment or office.

ex pacto illicito non oritur actio — no right of action may be based on an illicit agreement.

ex parte — from one side; describes proceedings where only one party has had the opportunity of being heard, eg proceedings for interim interdict. Cf *inter partes.*

ex pietate — from natural affection and duty.

ex post facto — from what is done afterwards; retrospective; effected so as to affect something already done.

ex proprio motu — of his own volition; of his own accord: describes a decision made by a judge without his being requested by a party to take that course.

ex turpi causa non oritur actio — no right of action arises from a disgraceful or immoral consideration.

ex vi aut metu — on grounds of force and fear. A deed granted under coercion may be reduced.

examination — the questioning of a witness, whether by the party calling him (examination-in-chief) or by an opposing party (cross-examination) or, following cross-examination, by the first party again (re-examination).

excambion — the exchange of one piece of immoveable property (land or buildings) for another piece of such property.

exceptio quae firmat legem exponit legem — an exception which confirms a law explains the law: a maxim of interpretation whereby the statement of an exception to a general rule implies the application of the rule in all other circumstances. Thus if the master of a ship is expressly prohibited from doing something otherwise lawful in his home port, that prohibition confirms that he may do it in a foreign port.

exception —
(1) an objection to a judge's charge in a civil jury trial which may be immediately considered by the judge or form the basis for review by the Inner House of the Court of Session;
(2) an obsolete term for a defence or defences, which survives in the plea *ope exceptionis* (qv).

Exchequer cause — a revenue matter heard by the Court of Session under jurisdiction derived from the former Court of Exchequer (qv).

exclusion clause. *See* **exemption clause**.

execution —
(1) the carrying out or enforcement of an order or decree of court;
(2) the written return or certificate that execution under (1) has been done;
(3) the act of authenticating a deed by signing it in accordance with the appropriate formalities;
(4) the carrying out of a sentence of death.

executor — a legal representative of a deceased person whose duty is to wind up the estate of the deceased.

executor dative — an executor appointed by the sheriff where no executor was nominated by the deceased or has accepted such appointment.

executor nominate — an executor nominated by the testator in his will.

executry — the process of winding up the estate of a deceased person in accordance with his will or with the law of intestate succession.

exempli gratia — for example; eg.

exemption clause *or* **exclusion clause** — a strictly construed clause in a contract providing that failure in performance by one party will not entitle the other to resile or claim damages. The effect of some such clauses was curtailed by the Unfair Contract Terms Act 1977.

exhibition — an action to compel the production of documents.

exoner — to release from further liability. Thus a judicial factor may ask for exoneration and discharge from the court.

expede — to draw up or complete and issue a document.

expenses — the costs of an action, including legal fees, outlays etc.

expose — to put up for sale by auction.

expressio (or enumeratio) unius est exclusio alterius — the special mention of one thing implies the exclusion of another: an important principle in the construction of statutes and deeds. Thus if a statute expressly provides for one or more methods of doing something, that provision implies the exclusion of some other method.

extortion —
(1) the crime of obtaining by means of unlawful threats money or some benefit not otherwise due;

(2) punitive terms in a contract which (except in certain circumstances relating to interest on loans) do not provide grounds for reduction of the contract.

extra commercium — excluded from commerce; used especially of things which may not be bought and sold, eg public roads and titles of honour.

extra-judicial — not carried out under judicial control; out of court. Thus extra-judicial expenses incurred outwith the normal course of judicial proceedings are not usually recoverable from the opponent by the successful party. A dispute which is being or might be heard by a court may be terminated by an extra-judicial settlement out of court.

extract —
(1) a formal copy of a decree or other judicial or legal document, duly certified as a true copy;
(2) to obtain such a formal copy with a view to enforcement.

extract decree — a formal certified copy of a decree which is used to enforce it. Thus to enforce a decree a party must first extract it.

extrinsic — from an external source, used especially of evidence so adduced to construe a statute or document as contrasted with interpretation from the text itself. Cf **intrinsic**.

f

facility and circumvention. *See* **circumvention**.

factor —
(1) a person who manages heritable property on behalf of the owner;
(2) an agent in possession of goods or their title who sells them, sometimes in his own name as apparent owner, for a principal on commission.
See also **judicial factor**.

factoring — the practice of a commercial agent who controls credit and debt collection for a principal or customer on commercial terms.

factory; factory and commission — a deed empowering another to act for the grantor in business transactions, eg buying and selling shares, similar to the English power of attorney.

factum praestandum. *See ad factum praestandum*.

faculty —
(1) a power which a person can exercise;
(2) a society of lawyers.

Faculty of Advocates — the society comprising the members of the Scottish Bar. *See also* **Dean of Faculty**.

falsa demonstratio non nocet — an erroneous description does not injure. The effectiveness of a provision in a deed is not affected by some error of description so long as there is no doubt as to the identity of the person or thing concerned.

falsehood, fraud and wilful imposition — the crime of obtaining by false pretences.

falsing the doom — questioning a legal decision; appealing.

fatal accident inquiry — an inquiry conducted by the sheriff and initiated by the procurator fiscal into any death which was sudden, suspicious or unexplained, or which occurred in circumstances giving rise to serious public concern.

feal and divot — a servitude which gives a right to cut turf for building, thatching or fuel.

fee —
(1) the right to and interest in heritable property, in contrast to liferent (qv);
(2) the remuneration of a lawyer or other professional person for his professional services.

fee fund — a fund into which court dues were paid by parties to proceedings in the Court of Session, and from which the administration of the court was in part financed.

ferae naturae — of a wild nature; describes wild or untamed animals, as distinct from animals *domitae naturae* (qv).

feu — a piece of land held by a feuar or vassal who pays feuduty, a perpetual rent, and who becomes the effective owner provided he observes the conditions of the feu. It is now incompetent to impose feuduties as a condition of granting land, and feuduties may now be redeemed, and must be redeemed upon transfer of the land.

feu farm *or* **feu ferme** — a hereditary feudal tenure (qv) under which land was formerly held by a vassal from a superior for a fixed money rent following an initial payment or *grassum*. Originally the vassal might be required to perform personal services (especially agricultural services), or pay rent in the form of cattle or grain. Feu ferme survived other forms of feudal tenure and these words are still used in modern grants in feu.

feuar — vassal. *See* **feu**.

feudal property. *See* **feu**.

feuduty. *See* **feu**.

fiar — the person in whom heritable property is vested (ie who holds the fee (qv)), in contrast to the liferenter, whose interest is a burden on that of the fiar.

fiars' prices — the annual prices of grain, until 1973 determined at the Fiars Court, on which some ministers' stipends were fixed. They were also used to fix skat duties in Orkney.

fiat ut petitur — let it be done as asked: a phrase used by a judge or magistrate granting a crave for a warrant.

fideicommissa — a trust to execute a testator's wishes.

fiduciary —
  (1) a person who holds something in trust (in contrast to a beneficiary), and who must not use his position to derive an unauthorised profit or advantage for himself;
  (2) property held in trust;
  (3) (adj) of the nature of a trust; held or given in trust.

filiation. *See* **affiliation**.

filius nullius — a bastard.

filum — a line. Thus *usque ad medium filum* means to the middle line of a stream or road.

fire-raising — setting fire to property. 'Wilful fire-raising' is intentional or deliberate (the equivalent of arson in English law), as distinct from negligent or accidental fire-raising.

firm — a partnership of persons carrying on a business.

first instance — describes a court before which or judge before whom a case is first heard, as distinct from a court or hearing a case on appeal.

first offender — a convicted person with no previous convictions.

fiscal —
  (1) relating to the national revenue;
  (2) shortened form of 'procurator fiscal' (qv).

fitted account — business accounts which have been drawn up by one party and docqueted as correct by the other, which raise a rebuttable presumption that all claims are settled.

fittings — moveable articles added, connected or attached to heritable property, which can be removed without causing damage (eg light bulbs and curtain rails). Contrast with fixtures (qv).

fixed security or charge — a security or charge affecting some specific property. Contrast with a floating charge (qv).

fixtures — moveable articles so added, connected or attached to heritable property that they cannot be removed without damage and so become part of it (eg baths and kitchen sinks). Contrast with fittings (qv).

flagranti delicto or flagranti crimine — in the act of committing a wrong or crime. Thus a criminal may be caught *in flagranti delicto*.

floating charge — a security for a debt or other obligation created by an incorporated company in favour of a creditor over all or part of its property, but enabling the company to continue to use the property until the charge becomes fixed. Contrast with fixed security (qv).

force and fear — coercion or duress such as may render an obligation void or voidable.

force majeure — something beyond the control of the parties to a contract, preventing its performance.

foreclosure — a remedy by which the ownership of security subjects is forfeited to the holder of the security by a debtor in default of payment.

forehand rent — rent agreed to be paid in advance, ie before the period of the lease to which it relates, as distinct from backhand rent (qv).

foreman — the spokesman for a jury.

forensic — of or used in courts of law, eg forensic medicine or forensic science.

foreshore — land lying between high and low watermarks of ordinary spring tides.

forisfamiliation — the emancipation of a minor from his family, by attaining majority, by marriage or by setting up an independent household.

forthcoming. *See* **furthcoming**.

fortiori. *See* *a fortiori*.

forum — a court or tribunal appropriate for the exercise of jurisdiction for a particular purpose.

forum non conveniens — a court or tribunal which is not appropriate, even though it may have jurisdiction.

fraud —
  (1) in the civil law, something said, done or omitted by one person with the intention of deceiving another to his detriment;
  (2) in criminal practice, the crime of false pretences which achieve some practical consequence.

fraudulent preference — *see* **unfair preference**.

fructus — fruits; produce grown on land.

fructus civiles — revenue; rents; interests; the produce of capital.

fructus industriales — agricultural produce raised by yearly sowing or planting.

fructus pecudum — produce of a flock (eg wool).

fructus pendentes — hanging or unpicked fruit. Cf *perceptio*.

fructus percepti; fructus separati — produce which has been picked or gathered. *See perceptio*.

fructus rei alienae — fruit or produce from another person's property.

fructus separati. *See fructus percepti*.

fugitive offender — a person accused of a crime or offence in one part of the Commonwealth, apprehended in another part and sent back to stand trial.

Full Bench — the High Court of Justiciary sitting with a greater number of judges (eg five, seven or nine) than the normal quorum of three for the hearing of appeals.

functus officio — having discharged one's official duty: the status of a judge or arbiter when he has decided the question brought before him. He may not review his own decision.

fund *in medio*. *See* **multiplepoinding**.

fungibles — moveables intended for consumption rather than use, and generally estimated by weight, number, volume or measure (eg foodstuffs).

furiosi nulla voluntas est — an insane person has no will.

furth of — out of, beyond the borders or limits of.

furthcoming *or* **forthcoming** — an action raised for the recovery of money or property arrested in the hands of a third person. *See* **arrestment**.

furtum — theft.

g

gable. *See* **mutual gable.**

game — wild animals or birds pursued and killed for sport or food. Different Game Acts regulating the rights of landowners and others to kill and take game define 'game' as including different species of creatures.

gaming — playing games of chance or chance and skill combined for winnings in money or money's worth, formerly illegal but now controlled by statute, and often requiring a licence. Gaming debts are not legally enforceable.

General Assembly — the highest court of the Church of Scotland, sitting annually in Edinburgh and presided over by the Moderator.

general disposition — a deed intended as a conveyance but which, because it lacks a full description of the land or proper feudal clauses, does not of itself constitute sufficient warrant to the disponee to obtain infeftment directly.

General Register of Sasines — a public register, maintained since the seventeenth century, in which all deeds transferring, creating or extinguishing rights to heritable property require to be recorded in order that they might have effect. The register is being progressively superseded by the Land Register of Scotland (qv).

general service. *See* **service** (3).

gift — a donation; a gratuitous transfer of heritable or moveable property to another.

glebe — a portion of land in a landward parish, generally near to the kirk or manse, which a minister has a right to use in addition to his stipend.

good faith. *See* ***bona fides.***

grant —
(1) a deed transferring property.
(2) to convey or transfer property to another.

grantee — one to whom a grant is made.

granter — one who makes a grant.

grassum — a single payment in addition to or in lieu of periodic payments (such as rent or feuduty), eg key money, or a part payment of rent paid in anticipation of entry.

gratuitous — without payment or other consideration.

gratuitous alienation — a gratuitous disposition of property by the owner to another.

Great Britain — Scotland, England and Wales, but not Northern Ireland.

ground annual — a non-feudal yearly duty chargeable on heritable property, the creation of which has been prohibited since 1974.

guarantee —
(1) a cautionary obligation (see **caution**);
(2) the responsibility of one person for actions of, or the truth of statements made by, another;
(3) a warranty by a manufacturer or retailer etc as to the quality etc of a product or service;
(4) to give such a warranty.

h

habile — admissible; valid; competent for a legal purpose.

habili modo — in the manner competent. Thus a proof *habili modo* is a proof competent in or appropriate to the circumstances.

habilis causa transferendi dominii — a *habile* or sufficient title for transferring ownership.

habit and repute —
  (1) a form of irregular marriage evidenced by lengthy cohabitation with the reputation of being married;
  (2) in the context of the crime of theft, it formerly implied the reputation of being a thief, and was an aggravation of the crime (now obsolete).

haereditas jacens — idle succession; succession to the estate of a deceased person which the executor or heir has not yet entered upon or taken up and which, as it still lies in the right of the deceased, is liable to be attached by diligence of creditors for his debts.

hamesucken — the crime of committing an assault upon a person in his own dwellinghouse after breaking into the house for that purpose. It is an aggravated assault, and was formerly a capital offence.

haver (pronounced 'havver') — a person who possesses a document required as evidence in court proceedings.

Health Service Commissioner for Scotland — the health service ombudsman in Scotland.

hearsay — evidence by a witness of what he has been told but has not himself seen or heard. It is generally incompetent, since statements made in court by a witness not based on his own knowledge are not normally admissible. It may, however, be used eg as an explanation or proof of a person's state of mind or in the context of *res gestae* (qv), and under the Civil Evidence (Scotland) Act 1988, hearsay evidence may be admitted in civil proceedings in appropriate circumstances.

heir — a person who succeeds to the property of a deceased person.

heir-apparent — one bound to succeed if he or she survives the deceased. Cf **apparent heir.**

heir-at-law; heir of line — until 1964 a person entitled to succeed to a deceased's heritable property under the rules of primogeniture, eg the eldest lawful son.

heir-female — the nearest heir of either sex who is related to the deceased only through a female.

heir-*in-mobilibus* — the next of kin or representative entitled to a deceased's moveable property on an intestacy.

heir-male — the nearest male relative who is related to the deceased only through a male.

heir-male of the body — the heir-male in direct line of descent.

heir of entail — a person entitled to succeed to entailed land. The title 'heir of entail' is retained after succession.

heir of line. *See* **heir-at-law.**

heir of provision; heir of tailzie — a person who succeeds by express provisions in eg a settlement.

heir of tailzie. *See* **heir of provision.**

heir of the body — a descendant who is alive at the death of the deceased.

heir-presumptive — the nearest heir at the moment, whose right may be defeated by the birth of a nearer heir.

heirs-portioner — formerly, when there was no male heir to heritage, the females in the same degree of relationship who succeeded in equal portions *pro indiviso*.

heritable property. *See* **heritage.**

heritage; heritable property — strictly, property passing to the heir-at-law of a deceased person. The Succession (Scotland) Act 1964 substantially assimilated rights of succession to heritable and moveable property. For historical reasons Scots law generally distinguished between heritable and moveable property, heritage being, in theory at any rate, concerned with the succession to land and its accessories. 'Heritage' and 'heritable property' continue to be used as synonyms for land and its pertinents generally. The ScottishLaw Commission has urged – so far without success – that property should be classified as immoveable and moveable.

heritor — a landowner, especially one formerly liable to contribute to the upkeep of a parish church.

High Court of Justiciary — the superior criminal court in Scotland, comprising the judges of the Court of Session in their capacity as Lords Commissioners of Justiciary, presided over by the Lord Justice-General. The court has original and appellate jurisdiction. No appeal lies from it to the House of Lords. The court is often referred to simply as 'the High Court'.

hinc inde — on this side; on that side: a term of art meaning 'on either side' or 'on this side and the other'. Thus the claims of parties *hinc inde* are their respective claims against each other.

hire purchase agreement — an agreement whereby goods are hired in return for periodical payments, the ownership of the goods passing to the hirer when specified conditions have been fulfilled.

holding —
  (1) land held under a lease for commercial agricultural purposes;
  (2) feudal tenure (see eg **base holding; blench; feu**).

holding out — words or actions whereby a person causes or allows the belief that he has a particular status such as that of an agent or partner. He may thereby attract to himself personal liability.

holograph — a document in which the essential words are written in the handwriting of the signatory or grantor, this (because of the difficulty of forging it) making it effective without witnesses to the signature. A typed deed may be 'adopted as holograph' if these words are written by the signatory in his own hand, but some deeds must have witnesses. Offers and acceptances for buying and selling heritable property, and covenants, are frequently adopted as holograph.

homicide — an act which, either directly or indirectly, or by natural consequence, takes away a person's life. *See* **casual homicide; culpable homicide; justifiable homicide; murder.**

homologation — an act approving, confirming, adopting or ratifying a deed or contract which in itself is otherwise defective.

honorarium — a form of financial gift as an acknowledgment for services. Counsel's fees have been so regarded as counsel may not sue for remuneration for their services.

horning. *See* **letters of horning.**

housebreaking — breaking into a building (whether a house or not): an aggravation of the crime of theft. It is not itself criminal unless undertaken for theft or with that intent.

humani nil a me alienum puto — I count nothing human unimportant to me: Terence. The motto of the Law Society of Scotland is '*Humani nihil alienum*'.

hypothec — a right in security given over the property of a debtor, although (unlike pledge or lien) the creditor does not have possession of the subjects, which remains with the debtor. Thus a landlord has a hypothec for rent over *invecta et illata* (qv).

i

IH — Inner House (qv).

I O U — a corruption of 'I owe you'; an acknowledgment of debt for a specific sum addressed to the creditor and signed by the debtor.

I P D. *See* **in praesentia Dominorum.**

id est — that is (abbreviated 'ie')

ignorantia juris neminem excusat — ignorance of the law excuses no-one.

illiquid — of an amount not yet fixed or ascertained.

impeachment —
(1) a formal allegation by a person accused of crime that another named person is guilty of it; otherwise known as incrimination, it constitutes a special defence (qv);
(2) formerly, a prosecution of an offender by the House of Commons, tried before the House of Lords.

imperitia enumeratur culpae — lack of skill is reckoned as a fault. Thus an employer is entitled to rely on an employee as having the ordinary skills of his trade.

impetrate — to obtain by request, especially by fraud or otherwise improperly.

impignorate — to pawn, pledge or mortgage.

implied — not stated or expressed. Used eg of a trust, an authority, a contract or a term of a contract which, in the particular circumstances, is deemed to exist notwithstanding an absence of express provision.

impotentia excusat legem — inability excuses failure to observe the law. The inability must be absolute and must not arise from the act or omission of the person making the plea.

improbation — an action to reduce a deed on the ground that it is forged.

improbative — not probative (qv).

improvement area — a declining industrial or commercial area so designated so as to allow the local authority to take measures to secure stable employment there.

improvement notice — a notice served by a health and safety inspector requiring that contraventions of health and safety provisions be remedied. Cf **prohibition notice.**

improvements — meliorations to leased subjects which go beyond mere repairs, which are not removeable from the subjects, and for which a tenant may be entitled to compensation from the landlord.

in absentia — in absence; undefended. Describes proceedings or a decree where no appearance or defence has been or was entered. Cf *in foro*.

in aemulationem vicini — to the injury or annoyance of a neighbour.

in arbitrio judicis — in the judge's discretion.

in articulo mortis — at the point of death.

in camera — in chambers; describes proceedings heard in the judge's room (and thus in private) as distinct from those heard in open court.

in causa — in the cause or the process.

in diem — as of a debt which is due but not yet prestable.

in dubio — in doubt; in a doubtful case or uncertain circumstances.

in eodem negotio — in the same business; arising out of the same matter or transaction.

in essentialibus — in the essential parts. An error in the essential parts of a deed or contract may render it liable to reduction.

in extenso — in full.

in facie ecclesiae — according to the rules of the church, as of a regular marriage solemnised in church.

in favorem — in favour of.

in flagrante delicto — in the act of committing a crime.

in forma pauperis — as a pauper. Before legal aid became available an indigent person might sue or defend *in forma pauperis* and be excused from paying agent's or counsel's fees and court expenses.

in forma specifica — in the form specified. Thus an equivalent will not suffice.

in foro — in court (a shortened form of *in foro contradictorio* or *in foro contensioso*: in a contested action); describes proceedings or a decree where an appearance or a defence has been entered. Contrast with *in absentia* (qv).

in fraudem — with fraudulent intention.

in gremio — in the body of, eg any clause or words contained in a deed or document.

in hoc statu — in this position or situation, a phrase which makes it clear that the matter concerned is being considered only in the light of the facts as known at the time, and without prejudice to review if further facts are subsequently disclosed.

in hunc effectum — for this purpose only

in integrum — entirely; to the fullest extent. Thus *restitutio in integrum* is restitution in full to the former state or condition.

in limine — on the threshold; describes a proposition stated at the outset eg of a legal argument or litigation.

in medio — in the middle, eg, in the context of multiplepoinding (qv), the fund *in medio*.

in modum probationis — in the form of or by way of proof.

in obligatione — by way of obligation.

in pari casu — in a similar position.

in pari causa potior est conditio possidentis — in an equal case, the possessor is in the better position. Thus any challenger must show a better title than the possessor has.

in pari delicto potior est conditio possidentis — in equal wrongdoing, the possessor or defender is in the better position. Thus a party to an illegal transaction may be unable to enforce a claim for the payment of money or delivery of goods otherwise due under that transaction.

in patiendo — in enduring or permitting. In the law relating to servitudes the servient proprietor is merely obliged to permit the dominant proprietor to exercise his rights, but need not help him as eg in maintaining a path or water pipe.

in personam — personally; describes a proceeding in which relief is sought against a specific person, as distinct from a proceeding *in rem*.

in praesentia Dominorum — in the presence of the Lords. The initials 'I P D' follow the signature of the presiding judge to an interlocutor or an Act of Sederunt of the Court of Session, indicating the presence of the other judges when he signs.

in quantum lucratus est — in so far as he has gained or profited: the measure of payment owed by the defender in a claim in recompense, where there is no claim under contract or implied contract.

in re communi melior est conditio prohibentis — in regard to property held in common, the position of the party prohibiting is the stronger.

in re mercatoria — in a mercantile transaction. In the interests of commerce, writings in mercantile transactions may be valid although lacking the solemnities of ordinary deeds.

in re propria — in one's own affairs.

in rem — regarding a thing; describes a proceeding in which relief is not sought against a specific person (*in personam*) but is sought as against the whole world in respect of some property or to establish title or status, or a right or claim in such circumstances.

in rem suam — regarding one's own property; to one's own advantage.

in retentis — among things kept back: describes evidence allowed to be taken and then laid aside until required, because it is in danger of being lost, eg where the witness is in extreme old age or is gravely ill or is about to leave the country.

in rixa — in the course of a quarrel. Words so spoken may not be actionable.

in solidum — for the whole. Several co-obligants bound *in solidum* are each liable to the creditor for full payment or performance, and the creditor may choose which to sue.

in toto — wholly; entirely.

in transitu — in transit. The Sale of Goods Act 1979 uses the English words, whereas the Sale of Goods Act 1893 used the Latin. In certain circumstances a creditor has a right to stop goods in transit.

in turpi causa potior est conditio possidentis — in a dispute involving an immoral purpose, the position of the possessor or defender is considered stronger.

in utero — in the womb; unborn. For certain purposes, if it is to the child's advantage, a child as yet unborn is deemed to have been born.

inaedificatum solo cedit solo — anything built on the ground belongs to the ground; more accurately, and subject to many exceptions, it belongs to the owner of the ground.

incapax —
  (1) (adj) not capable; having legal, mental or physical incapacity;
  (2) (n) a person who is *incapax*.

incest — crime of sexual intercourse between persons within specified relationships: see the Incest and Related Offences (Scotland) Act 1986.

inchoate — undeveloped or incomplete and therefore ineffective.

incompetent —
(1) describes an action or any procedure which the court does not have power to entertain;
(2) a preliminary plea to the foregoing effect;
(3) describes a witness whose evidence, or evidence which, is not admissible.

incorporation — the formation of individuals or other legal entities into a separate legal entity, distinct in law from its constituent members, eg a public limited company or a local authority.

incorporeal — describes property or rights which are not tangible and which have no physical existence, eg an annuity, copyright, patent or stocks and shares.

incrimination. *See* **impeachment** (1).

incumbrance — a burden on heritable property.

indebiti solutio — the payment of something not due. Money paid under the erroneous belief that there is liability to pay it may be recoverable. See *condictio indebiti.*

indemnity — an undertaking given by one person to protect another from damage or loss that might otherwise have to be suffered.

indenture — a deed made by several parties, now mainly concerned with instruction and apprenticeship. It was so called because the edges of the several copies were cut in a distinct pattern so that each copy corresponded with the others.

independent contractor — a person engaged by another to perform work or service but not as an employee.

indictment — a written accusation of serious crime in the name of the Lord Advocate. Procedure on indictment is called 'solemn procedure', and, whether trial is in the High Court or the sheriff court, the judge sits with a jury of fifteen, whose decision to convict may be reached by a simple majority.

indorse *or* **endorse** — to write on the back of a document, eg a cheque or bill of exchange.

induciae — a pause; a truce; days of grace allowed in legal proceedings for a person to perform some act, eg for a defender to enter appearance, or for a debtor to pay before diligence can proceed on a decree.

industrial — produced by a person's labour, eg cultivated crops as distinct from crops growing wild.

industrial tribunal — a statutory tribunal comprising a legally-qualified chairman appointed by the Lord President and two lay members appointed by the Secretary of State for Employment and representing employers and employed persons, with jurisdiction in respect of unfair dismissal, redundancy payments, discrimination and other questions relating to employment.

infant; *infans* — not strictly a term of art in Scots law, but may be used in the Roman law sense to indicate a child who has not reached its eighth birthday. Confusion has sometimes resulted in applying to Scotland United Kingdom legislation where the draftsman used the term 'infant' in the English sense as comprehending those under the age of majority. *See also* **minor.**

infeftment — investment of title to heritage in a new owner, formerly by symbolically giving him sasine or possession by delivery of earth and stone, now by recording the deed in the General Register of Sasines or the Land Register of Scotland (qv).

infer — to deduce a fact by reasoning from the existence of one or more other facts.

ingather — to get in money or other property due to eg executors or trustees.

inhibition — an order by the Court of Session, called 'letters of inhibition', forbidding a debtor to burden or part with heritage to the prejudice of a creditor.

initial writ — the document by which an action is begun in the sheriff court, equivalent to the summons in the Court of Session.

injuria — a legal wrong generally or, more specifically, insult.

injuria non excusat injuriam — one wrong does not excuse another. One is not entitled to take the law into one's own hands.

injuria non praesumitur — wrong is not presumed. Just as guilt of a crime is not presumed, so also a civil wrong must be proved by whoever complains of it.

Inner House — that part of the Court of Session, comprising two permanent Divisions (qv), which is primarily concerned with the court's appellate jurisdiction. Originally the Inner House lay further away from the courthouse entrance than did the Outer House (qv).

innominate contract — a contract which does not fall into one of the established nominate categories of contract (eg sale or agency). If the contract is not merely innominate but is also unusual and anomalous, it must generally be proved by the writ or oath of the defender.

insolvency — the state of being unable to pay one's debts. *See also* **apparent insolvency.**

insolvency practitioner — in the law of bankruptcy and insolvency, a person qualified to act as a liquidator, administrator or supervisor in relation to a company or an individual: see the Insolvency Act 1986, s 388.

insolvent —
(1) unable to pay one's debts;
(2) a person who is unable to pay his debts.

instance — the part of a writ or summons which names and designates the parties to the action.

institute (n) —
(1) the person first named in a destination of property, as contrasted with a person named as entitled if the institute fails (the 'substitute' (qv));
(2) an institutional writing (qv).

institutional writings — literary works, judicially recognised as authoritative sources of law, which deal comprehensively with Scots civil or criminal law, and follow the style and structure of the *Institutes* of Justinian. Examples include works of Stair, Bankton, Erskine and Bell.

instruct —
(1) to appoint and authorise a solicitor or advocate to provide professional legal services and provide him with the necessary information on which he is to act;
(2) to supply evidence or documentary proof of a fact.

instrument — a formal legal deed or document.

inter partes — between parties; describes proceedings at which each party is present or represented. Cf *ex parte.*

inter se — between two or more persons or things.

inter vivos — between living persons; describes deeds or legal acts intended to take effect during the granter's lifetime. Cf *mortis causa.*

interdict —
(1) a judicial remedy granted by a court forbidding an act or course of action (in England, an injunction);
(2) to obtain such a remedy against a person.

interim — meantime; temporary.

interim Act — an Act of the General Assembly of the Church of Scotland in force only till the next General Assembly.

interim interdict — a temporary interdict granted by the court on an *ex parte* application for a limited period until both sides can be heard.

interim trustee — an insolvency practitioner (qv) appointed by the Court of Session or the sheriff to safeguard a debtor's estate and generally administer the sequestration process pending the election of the permanent trustee (qv).

interlocutor — the official and effective expression of an order or judgment pronounced by the court in the course of a civil action. Interlocutors are signed by the presiding judge and entered on interlocutor sheets which form part of the process (qv).

intermeddling — unjustified interference.

interpretation clause — a clause in a deed setting forth the special meanings of words for the purposes of that deed.

interpretation section — a section in an Act of Parliament setting forth the special meanings of words for the purposes of that Act.

interrogatories — written questions, judicially approved, which are put to witnesses examined under a commission (qv).

interruption — a step legally required to stop the running of a period of prescription or limitation.

intestate —
    (1) a person who dies without having left a valid will;
    (2) describes such a person or his estate.

intra fines commissi — within the limits of the commission or trust. Describes an act within the express or implied authority of eg a servant or agent.

intra vires — within the power. Describes an act which is within the power or authority of the person who does it. Cf *ultra vires.*

intrinsic — from an internal source, used especially of evidence of interpretation derived from the text of a deed itself. Cf **extrinsic.**

intromission — the act of handling or dealing with funds or other property of another person. Thus an executor intromits with the property of the deceased. If unauthorised, the intromission is vitious intromission.

intrusion — the delict of entering into possession of heritable property without any title in the person entering, albeit without violence.

invecta et illata — things imported, brought or carried in; the moveable effects of a tenant brought onto leased premises which are subject to the landlord's hypothec (qv) as security for rent.

inventory —
    (1) a list of the property of a deceased person sworn to and lodged in court by an executor;
    (2) a list of the contents of a house etc made up at the beginning of a furnished let.

inventory of process — a list of documents in a process (qv) which must be lodged in duplicate in court along with them.

inventory of productions — a list of productions in a civil action, which must be lodged in process (qv) along with the productions.

investiture — infeftment (qv).

ipso facto — by the fact itself.

ipso jure — by operation of law.

irregular marriage — a marriage by parties with requisite legal capacity but without the formalities for a regular marriage. Cohabitation for a material period with the habit and repute of being married constitutes now the only recognised form of irregular marriage, though irregular marriages by other forms prior to 1 July 1940 are recognised.

irritancy — the forfeiture of a right, usually in feudal or leasehold property, through failure to observe, or contravention of, the law (legal irritancy) or an agreement (conventional irritancy). Enforcement requires a court decree.

irritancy clause — a clause in an agreement providing that the agreement will be void if some condition in it is contravened.

irritate —
    (1) to make void; to nullify;
    (2) to enforce an irritancy (qv).

ish — issue; the date of termination or expiry of a lease.

islands area — one of the three areas into which the Scottish islands are divided for local government purposes. The local authority is the islands council.

issue —
    (1) all direct descendants of a person;
    (2) the formal question for decision put to a jury in a civil action;
    (3) more loosely, a question for decision in a court.

iter — a rural servitude allowing a person a right of way to pass over the land of another on horse or on foot.

j

J P — justice of the peace (qv).

jedge — a gauge or means of verifying a standard measure.

jedge and warrant — an order given by the Dean of Guild prior to 1975 authorising the repair or rebuilding of dilapidated houses, the expense of which became a real burden on the property.

joint adventure — a partnership confined to one particular transaction, speculation, course of trade or voyage.

joint and several obligation — an obligation resting upon more than one person in which each obligant is liable for performance jointly or collectively with the others but also severally or individually. Thus the creditor in such an obligation may sue all or, alternatively, any one of his debtors.

joint obligation — an obligation in which each co-obligant is liable only for his share of the debt.

joint property — property in which ownership is indivisibly vested in two or more persons. Each cannot dispose of any share as there are no shares. Examples include property of the members of a members' club (qv) and an estate vested in trustees. The interest of a deceased joint owner passes to the survivors. Cf **common property**.

joint stock company — a business organisation the stock or capital of which was contributed jointly by a number of persons. Since the seventeenth century the liability of those involved could be limited to their contributed capital. In the nineteenth century the joint stock company gradually developed into the modern limited company.

joint wrongdoers — two or more persons who have contributed either equally or in varying proportions to the commission of a delict. They have a joint and several obligation (qv) to make reparation for loss or damage caused thereby.

judex non reddit plus quam quod petens ipse requirit — a judge cannot give more than the petitioner himself asks.

judex tenetur impertiri judicium suum — a judge is bound to give the benefit of his decision. Thus a judge must do his duty and reach a decision on a case properly brought before him.

judge — a person appointed to consider and determine cases brought before the courts.

judge advocate — an officer appointed to advise courts-martial (qv) on matters of procedure, law and evidence. He reports the proceedings of courts-martial to the Judge Advocate General, an officer appointed by the Lord Chancellor as adviser to the army and air force in relation to courts-martial and military and air force law. Similar arrangements apply in respect of naval courts-martial, the officer appointed by the Lord Chancellor being the Judge Advocate of the Fleet.

judgment — the final determination in a litigation in which the judge sets forth his decision and, usually, his reasons for reaching it.

judgment roll. *See* **rolls**.

judicia posteriora sunt in lege fortiora — later judgments are stonger in law: a rule on the application of precedents. Thus the latest judgment on a controversial question of law, even though it follows a number of earlier contrary decisions, is binding on judges in inferior courts.

Judicial Committee of the Privy Council — a tribunal of senior judges appointed to hear appeals competently brought before the sovereign in Council. The committee does not hear appeals from ordinary United Kingdom courts. Its jurisdiction is now restricted to appeals from the courts of the diminishing list of British colonies and dependencies, certain ecclesiastical and admiralty appeals and appeals under certain statutes, eg those relating to the medical and allied professions.

judicial examination —
  (1) formerly the initial interrogation by a magistrate or sheriff of a person charged with serious crime, but latterly the first formal appearance of such a person before a sheriff when the accused may, if he wishes, make a declaration (qv);
  (2) since 1980 the questions which the procurator fiscal may put to such an accused about the charge at that appearance (Criminal Procedure (Scotland) Act 1975, s 20A).

judicial factor — a person appointed by a court to hold or administer property in Scotland where it is in dispute or where there is no one who could properly control or administer it. A judicial factor must find caution, and his work is supervised by the Accountant of Court (qv).

judicial reference — the reference, with the court's approval, by the parties to an existing litigation of the whole or some part of the matter in dispute to an arbiter or referee.

judicial review — a remedy available in the Court of Session whereby the actings or decisions of inferior courts, tribunals and other public officers and authorities can be brought under review, on the ground of illegality, irrationality or procedural impropriety, where no other form of appeal is available. Power is similarly available to compel such bodies to act where they have improperly failed so to do.

judicial sale — the sale of property authorised by a court in certain situations, eg of goods seized by poinding or land subject to heritable security.

judicial separation — an order of court, short of divorce (which would permit remarriage), separating spouses *a mensa et thoro* (qv), thus allowing them to live permanently apart. An action for judicial separation is usually accompanied by a claim for aliment (qv). A decree of judicial separation does not preclude later proceedings for divorce.

judiciary — the collective name for all the professional judges in the country.

judicis est judicare secundum allegata et probata — it is the part or duty of the judge to decide in accordance with what has been alleged and proved. Thus judgment must proceed upon what has been proved in the case.

judicis est jus dicere non jus dare — it is the part or duty of the judge to express the law, not to make it. A judge is required to administer and decide the law. He must not himself purport to legislate.

judicium semper pro veritate accipitur — a judgment is always accepted as true. Thus, subject to any competent appeal, a judgment pronounced by a court upon a matter properly submitted to it for decision is conclusive as between the parties, both on the facts and on the law involved.

junior counsel — an advocate who has not been appointed Queen's Counsel (qv).

jurisdiction —
  (1) in international law, the power of the state to enact and enforce legislation;
  (2) the authority of a court to entertain and determine a particular case, an authority which may be circumscribed by territorial boundaries, the value or type of case or other considerations, and which, in civil proceedings, is now primarily determined by EEC rules set forth in the Civil Jurisdiction and Judgments Act 1982;
  (3) the territorial area within which a particular court may exercise that authority.

jurisprudence — theoretical (especially philosophical and sociological) studies of law in general, are in particular systems of law.

jurist — a very learned lawyer. The term is normally applied to well-recognised and respected legal writers, scholars and philosophers.

juristic person — an artificial entity with legal capacity, rights and liabilities (eg a corporation), as distinct from a natural person (qv).

jury — a group of lay persons chosen from among the local population to hear and consider the evidence in legal proceedings and decide (under the judge's directions on law) the issues of fact. In Scotland a jury of fifteen persons can reach a verdict in criminal trials unanimously or, in case of guilt, by a simple majority of at least eight.

jus accrescendi praefertur oneribus — the right of survivorship is preferred to burdens. Thus one of the proprietors of joint property cannot burden it to the detriment of the survivor or survivors.

jus ad rem — the right to a thing; a personal right (or *jus in personam*) to property under a particular obligation, enforceable against the obligant, contrasted with a real right (or *jus in re*) in the property, enforceable against all. For example, the purchaser of a house has a personal right (*jus ad rem*) to it under missives. When he records or registers the disposition in his favour, he has a real right (*jus in re*) to it.

jus administrationis — right to administer: the former right enjoyed by a husband to administer his wife's property and to validate her acts with his consent.

jus civile — civil law or Roman law. *See* **civil law**.

jus cogens — a statutory or contractual provision stipulating a mandatory legal consequence. Cf *jus dispositivum*.

jus coronae — the right of the Crown; the right under which the Crown may claim those things said to be under regalia. *See* **regalia**.

jus crediti — the right of credit, ie of a creditor; an enforceable right in property, often contrasted with mere expectancy, eg the right of a beneficiary in property held in trust for his behoof.

jus dispositivum — a statutory or contractual provision the stipulated consequences of which may be averted by agreement between the persons concerned. Cf *jus cogens*.

jus dominio proximum — a right of almost, but not quite, absolute property, eg that of one who holds land in feu.

jus exigendi — the right to require immediate fulfilment of an obligation.

jus gentium — the law of nations; international law.

jus in personam — a personal right, contrasted with real right: *see* *jus ad rem*.

jus in re — a right in a thing. *See* *jus ad rem*.

jus mariti — the right of a husband: the former right under which a husband acquired absolutely the personal property of his wife.

jus pascendi pecoris — the right of pasturing cattle, one of the rural servitudes.

jus pignoris — the right of pledge; the right of a creditor, holding a pledge as security for the performance of an obligation, to keep it until the obligation is fulfilled.

jus possidendi — the right to possess or occupy.

jus quaesitum tertio — a right acquired by a third party in consequence of a stipulation in his favour expressed in a contract between other parties.

jus relictae — the right of the widow; a widow's right to one-third or one-half of her deceased husband's free moveable property, the proportion depending upon whether or not he leaves children or issue of predeceasing children. The *jus relictae* is calculated after deduction of debts and expenses, and any statutory prior rights if the deceased died intestate. A widower has a similar right, the *jus relicti*.

jus representationis — the right of representation; the right by which a descendant or other relative succeeds to the rights and privileges of a deceased person in accordance with the law of succession.

jus tertii — the right of a third party: a plea against an argument maintained by one who has no title or interest to advance it. The argument belongs to the third party.

jus utendi et abutendi — the right of using and consuming, the essence of ownership. The proprietor can not only use his property; he may destroy it by consuming it. Cf *jus utendi fruendi*.

jus utendi fruendi — the right of using and enjoying, the characteristic of a liferent. The use and enjoyment must be consistent with full preservation of the subject. Cf *jus utendi et abutendi*.

jusiurandum — an oath.

justice of the peace — a lay person appointed by the Secretary of State for Scotland, on the advice of a local committee, to preside as judge in the district court, to administer oaths and to exercise other miscellaneous powers.

Justiciar — the ancient name for the officer of state who became the highest criminal judge in Scotland, now known as the Lord Justice-General.

Justiciary. *See* **High Court of Justiciary**.

justifiable homicide — killing while exercising a private right, eg of self-defence, or a public duty, eg execution of sentence of death.

justo tempore — in due time; at the right time.

k

Keeper of the Records of Scotland — the officer responsible for the Scottish Record Office in which are preserved the public records of Scotland, including records of government departments in Scotland, Scottish courts and other public bodies, and for the Scottish Records Advisory Service, which advises the Secretary of State and the Lord President of the Court of Session on questions relating to Scottish public records.

Keeper of the Registers of Scotland — the officer responsible for the Department of the Registers of Scotland, in which are maintained the General Register of Sasines, the Land Register of Scotland, and registers of a wide range of deeds relating to succession, trusts, family agreements and state appointments.

Keeper of the Rolls — the Principal Clerk of Session in the capacity in which he keeps the rolls of the Court of Session and supervises the listing of all proceedings therein.

Keeper of the Signet — the titular head, appointed by the Crown, of the Society of Writers to the Signet. All summonses in the Court of Session originally required to be prepared and subscribed by clerks in the royal Secretariat of State which controlled the king's personal seal or Signet. All warrants for service of summonses and charges to implement the court's decrees required to be sealed with the Signet, and in that process were said to 'pass the Signet'. The clerks of the Secretariat are now members of the Society of Writers to the Signet. The effective head of the society is the Deputy Keeper of the Signet, a senior member of the society appointed by the Keeper.

kindly tenant — a person who holds land under a hereditary lease as distinct from a feudal charter. The tenancy is constituted by entry in the landlord's rent book, and is designed to preserve ancient rights to land. It now survives only at Lochmaben, where the right may be transferred to strangers.

kirk session — a church court consisting of the minister and elders of a parish church adhering to the presbyterian form of church government. It is also recognised in regiments such as the Black Watch. It has administrative as well as pastoral functions.

l

L J-C — Lord Justice-Clerk (qv).

L P — Lord President (qv).

L S — *locus sigilli* (the place of the seal): the letters may be found printed within a circle on documents to indicate the place where a personal seal used to be affixed.

label — a physical production, as distinct from a document, in a criminal trial, so-called because there is usually affixed to it a label bearing the signatures of witnesses who have identified it and are expected to identify it again at the trial.

labes realis quae rei inhaeret — a real blemish which attaches to the thing itself: a fundamental defect in the title to property so that no-one may acquire right thereto except the original owner. Thus stolen property continues to be incapable of lawful acquisition even by a purchaser in good faith.

lacuna —
  (1) an omission or blank space in a document;
  (2) a situation not covered by a statutory provision.

laesio enormis. *See* **enorm lesion**.

Lammas — a quarter day in Scotland (1 August).

Land Register of Scotland — a public register of interests in land in Scotland under the management and control of the Keeper of the Registers of Scotland. It is being brought progressively into effect under the Land Registration (Scotland) Act 1979. It will eventually supersede the recording of deeds in the General Register of Sasines (qv).

land tenure — the system under which land is held. In Scotland it is mainly feudal in principle, but still udal in parts of Orkney and Shetland, these islands having been formerly under Norwegian rule. Church land and land acquired by compulsory acquisition may be held on allodial title.

landlord — the party to the contract of lease who grants the lease; the proprietor of heritable property which is the subject of a lease.

Lands Tribunal for Scotland — the tribunal established under the Lands Tribunal Act 1949 to determine referred disputes relating to compensation on compulsory acquisition, the removal or variation of conditions in the title to land and other matters arising out of the use of land in Scotland.

Lands Valuation Appeal Court — a court comprising three judges of the Court of Session determining appeals from local valuation appeal committees. Normally one judge forms a quorum.

landward — until 1975 described that part or area of a county lying outside the boundaries of burghs.

last heir. *See* **ultimus haeres**.

lata culpa aequiparatur dolo — gross fault is held to be equivalent to fraud.

lato sensu — in a broad or wide sense.

law agent — the traditional Scottish term used to describe a solicitor, often abbreviated to 'agent'. The English usage 'solicitor' has been recognised in modern Scottish legislation and is now in general use.

Law Commission. *See* **Scottish Law Commission**.

law reports — reports of decisions of the courts published for information and reference. *See also* **precedent**.

Law Society of Scotland — a statutory body created in 1949 comprising all practising solicitors in Scotland. It controls admission to and discipline within the profession. The existing societies of solicitors such as the Writers to the Signet, the Royal Society of Procurators in Glasgow and the Society of Advocates in Aberdeen were not superseded on the institution of the Law Society of Scotland, but their members also belong to the new statutory professional body.

lawburrows — an action by which a person who has good grounds for fearing that another person may damage his person or property may secure a court order requiring that other to find caution or security to keep the complainer harmless from illegal violence.

lead evidence — to call witnesses to give evidence; to adduce evidence.

leader — the senior counsel for a party in a case. He is usually a Queen's Counsel.

leading case — an important judicial precedent.

leading question — a question which suggests the answer. It is not permitted in court except in cross examination.

lease —
  (1) the hiring of heritable property (or, more recently, moveable property, especially vehicles and commercial or industrial equipment) by a lessor to a lessee for a specified period and on prescribed conditions, usually for the payment of rent;
  (2) the formal document giving effect to such a lease;
  (3) to hire on a lease.

leasing–making — the obsolete crime of verbal sedition involving contemptuous defamation of the sovereign or the Prince of Scotland.

legacy — a bequest of money or moveable property to a beneficiary conferred by the will of a deceased person.

legal (n) — the period of ten years allowed to a debtor to redeem his heritable property after adjudication (qv). If he fails to pay the debt within the legal, his right to redeem may be foreclosed by action for declarator of expiry of the legal.

legal aid — professional legal advice or representation provided under a statutory scheme to persons of limited means but who may be required to contribute to its cost.

legal interest — interest which is, in limited circumstances, due to be paid *ex lege* or according to the law.

legal person — a natural individual person or an artificial entity with legal capacity, rights and duties.

legal rights — rights to share in the estate of a deceased person, enjoyed by a surviving spouse and issue, regardless of any will. See also *jus relictae*, **legitim** and **prior rights**.

legal tender — cash in which a debt must be paid. A creditor is technically entitled to insist upon payment of a debt in legal tender, which in Scotland includes most current coins and Bank of England notes of a denomination of less than £5. Scottish banknotes are not legal tender. Since the withdrawal of £1 Bank of England notes no notes are now legal tender in Scotland.

legatum per universitatem — a universal legacy; a legacy of the testator's whole estate.

legatum rei alienae — the legacy of a subject not belonging to the testator but to some other person. If the testator mistakenly believed the subject to be his, the bequest is ineffective. If he knew that it was not his, the executors must try to acquire it for the legatee or otherwise satisfy him.

legatum universitatis — a universal legacy; a legacy of the testator's whole estate.

legislation — laws enacted by Parliament (ie the Scots Parliament before 1 May 1707, the Parliament of Great Britain from 1707 to 1800, and the Parliament of the United Kingdom thereafter); and, since 1973, legal acts of the EC Council or the EC Commission. Orders in Council, statutory instruments, regulations and rules made by ministers under the authority of an Act of Parliament are known as subordinate legislation.

legitim — a legal right to a share in the moveable estate of a deceased ancestor, which vests in any surviving lawful issue *ipso jure*, sometimes called the 'bairns part'. Illegitimate children are now also entitled to legitim. The legitim fund is either one-third or one-half of the deceased's estate: one-third if there is a surviving spouse entitled to his or her 'legal rights', and one-half if there is no surviving spouse or a surviving spouse has renounced those rights. If the deceased died intestate a surviving spouse is entitled to certain prior rights which rank after claims by creditors of the deceased and are deducted before legal rights such as legitim are calculated.

legitimation *per subsequens matrimonium* — the legitimation of a person born out of wedlock by the subsequent marriage of his parents.

lenocinium — pandering to licentiousness: connivance by a husband in his wife's infidelity, affording a defence to an action for divorce brought by the husband and founded on that adultery.

leonina societas — a leonine partnership: a form of partnership in which one partner bears all the loss while another receives all the profit (the lion's share). It is not recognised in Scots law, but the phrase is used generally of a partnership said to be void or otherwise illegal.

lesion — loss or injury. *See* **enorm lesion**.

lessor and **lessee** — the landlord and the tenant, the parties to a lease.

letter of request — a request to a foreign court or tribunal for the examination of a witness resident abroad or the production or examination of other evidence. The letter may be obtained on application to the Court of Session or the sheriff in civil causes and, since 1980, to the High Court of Justiciary or the sheriff in criminal proceedings.

letters — a writ or warrant by a court. Formerly more common than in current practice.

letters of arrestment — a writ to attach the property of a debtor in the hands of a third person as security against the debtor. *See* **arrestment**.

letters of caption — an obsolete warrant to arrest for debt, finally abolished by the Debtors (Scotland) Act 1987.

letters of horning — an obsolete mode of diligence whereby a debtor under a court order was charged to pay his debt on pain of being 'put to the horn'. If he defaulted, a court officer blew three blasts of a horn at the local market cross and denounced the debtor as an outlaw, whereupon his moveable property was forfeited to the Crown. Letters of horning were finally abolished by the Debtors (Scotland) Act 1987.

letters of inhibition. *See* **inhibition**.

letters of open doors — a warrant authorising the opening of a lockfast place (qv) in order to poind subjects held therein.

letters of second diligence — a warrant authorising the apprehension and detention, until he finds caution, of a witness who has failed or, it is reasonably suspected, will fail upon citation to attend court to give evidence.

leviora delicta — the lighter delicts: petty crimes and offences which may be tried summarily, as distinguished from the more serious crimes which are tried before a jury under solemn procedure (qv).

Lex Aquilia — an important Roman law which, as developed by the later civilians, provided the basis for the fundamental principle of liability for damage to the person or to property. It is the basis of much of the Scots law of delict.

lex contractus — the law of the contract. This may include stipulations which differ from the provisions of the common law or statute law but which are not illegal or immoral and which the law will therefore enforce.

lex domicilii — the law of the domicile. The personal law of an individual may be governed by the law of his domicile or the law of his nationality. *See also* **domicile**.

lex fori — the law of the court; the law of the country in which litigation takes place, and which regulates matters such as evidence, court procedure and diligence.

lex loci actus — the law of the place where the act was performed.

lex loci contractus — the law of the place where the contract was made or concluded. This law may be relevant in determining the proper law of the contract, its formal validity and the capacity of the parties. Cf *lex loci solutionis*.

lex loci deliciti — the law of the place where a crime was committed.

lex loci rei sitae — the law of the place where the subject (usually heritable) is situated.

lex loci solutionis — the law of the place of payment; the law of the place where the contract is to be performed. Cf *lex loci contractus*.

lex nil frustra facit — the law does nothing in vain. Thus the court will not pronounce a useless or impractical decree, for example it will refuse a simple declarator of an abstract inconsequential fact or an interdict where no wrong has been committed or threatened.

lex non cogit ad impossibilia — the law does not compel the performance of what is impossible.

lex non requirit verificari quod apparet curiae — the law does not require proof of what is apparent to the court. For example, the court can see for itself whether a deed has been stamped.

lex posterior derogat priori — a later statute derogates from a prior one: a maxim of interpretation that the later of two mutually inconsistent enactments prevails.

lex semper dabit remedium — the law will always afford a remedy for every wrong of which it can or does take notice.

lex talionis — the law of retaliation; the rule of Mosaic law that punishment be analogous to the crime, ie an eye for an eye and a tooth for a tooth (*Deut* 19:21). It has never been part of the law of Scotland.

libel —
(1) a written defamatory statement (an English term now loosely used in Scotland, though Scots law does not distinguish between libel and slander in defamation, as does English law);
(2) a statement of a criminal charge;
(3) to defame in writing;
(4) to set forth a criminal charge.

liberation — release from custody, detention or imprisonment.

liberis nascituris — to children yet to be born. Certain legal rights may be conferred, especially in marriage contracts, on children yet unborn.

licence —
(1) a permit to do what otherwise could not lawfully be done (eg drive a vehicle on a road, sell intoxicating liquor, take and kill game or possess firearms);
(2) the document constituting that permit;
(3) a contractual right, falling short of what is recognised as a legal tenancy, to use or occupy the heritable property of another;
(4) to grant such a permit, document or right.

licensing board — a board, comprising members of a district or islands council, established under the Licensing (Scotland) Act 1976 to consider and determine applications for licences to sell alcoholic liquor.

liege —
(1) (adj) bound by feudal tenure;
(2) (n) a subject of the reigning monarch.

liege poustie (n) (perhaps derived from *legitima potestas*) — the state of sufficient health in which a person can validly and effectively dispose, *mortis causa* or otherwise, of heritable property (an obsolete phrase).

lien (pronounced 'lee-en') — a right to retain a debtor's moveable property until he has paid his debt. The right, which Scots law acquired from England, applies particularly to commercial situations.

liferent (pronounced 'life rent') — the right to use and enjoy during a lifetime the property of another, without consuming its substance. 'Proper liferents', which are rare in modern practice, involve only liferenter and fiar, and the right enjoyed by the liferenter is of the nature of a personal servitude. When the fee is vested in trustees and the liferenter has only a trust liferent, the liferent is described as an 'improper liferent'. Liferents may be created by reservation, as where the granter gives the fee while retaining the liferent; or by constitution, when he grants a liferent while retaining the fee or disposing of it to another.

light — a servitude, which must be constituted in writing, which restrains the proprietor of the servient tenement, by building or otherwise, from obstructing the light of the dominant tenement.

limitation period — the period within which an action or claim must be raised in court. If an action is raised out of time the claim will normally be barred.

limited liability — the principle whereby the liability of the contributors of capital to a commercial undertaking for losses incurred by that undertaking is limited, for each individual contributor, to the actual amount of the capital introduced by him. The principle forms the fundamental basis for the development of the joint stock company (qv) and the limited company.

limited partnership — a partnership where one or more general partners are liable for all the partnership debts and obligations, and one or more limited partners are liable for those debts and obligations only to the extent of their contribution to the partnership assets: see the Limited Partnership Act 1907, s 4(2).

lining — the measuring or tracing out of the boundaries of holdings of land, especially in burghs. A decree of lining was an order of the Dean of Guild authorising building works within the burgh in conformity with statutory or customary requirements.

liquid (adj) — of a certain, fixed and ascertained or instantly ascertainable amount.

liquidate damages — damages provided for in a contract as the parties' estimate of the loss which will result from breach. These are consequently recoverable in the event of breach without proof of actual loss.

liquidation — the procedure for winding up and dissolving a limited company. It may be voluntary, if agreed upon by the shareholders, or judicial, if ordered by a court. See the Insolvency Act 1986.

liquidator — the person appointed in a liquidation (qv) to ingather the assets of a company and settle and adjust the claims of its creditors.

lis alibi pendens — a suit pending elsewhere: a defence, constituting a preliminary defence, that the same question as that raised in the action is already the subject of litigation depending between the parties in another court of competent jurisdiction. If that court is outside Scotland, the court may at its discretion sist the action in Scotland until the other action is determined.

lis est finita *or* **lis est sopita** — the case is finished. Not only is the action ended but its subject matter is finally determined. Where, for example, a case has been referred to the defender's oath and he commits perjury in denying liability, he may be prosecuted for the perjury but, as regards the civil action, *lis est sopita*.

lis pendens — a pending action or petition. *See* **pendente lite**.

litem suam facere — to make the suit his own. A judge was said to make the suit his own where, through corruption, malice, fear or favour or even, sometimes, through ignorance of the law, he made the wrong judgment. However, acts done by a judge, including a sheriff in his judicial capacity, are absolutely privileged and cannot be made the subject of an action for damages.

litigiosity — the implied prohibition of the alienation of heritable property which defeats an action or diligence to acquire the property. Land is rendered litigious on inhibition or on the service of a summons in certain proceedings relating to land.

litiscontestation — the stage of an action at which issue is joined by the lodging of defences, and at which, consequently, the action becomes contested.

loan — a contract whereby the lender gives money or moveable property to the borrower for his temporary use. Species of loan include *commodatum* (qv) and *mutuum* (qv).

local authority — a statutory body of councillors, elected as a council by local voters, with extensive statutory administrative powers, functions and duties, especially over services within its area. In Scotland local authorities comprise regional, islands and district councils.

local valuation appeal committee — a committee, comprising members of a local valuation panel, constituted for a valuation area to hear and determine appeals and complaints under the Acts relating to the valuation of land.

locatio; **location** — hire of premises, goods or services; derived from Roman law *locatio conductio*, the categories of which are adopted into the terminology of Scots law: see the entries which follow.

locatio custodiae — the hire of the custody of a thing, ie the contract of deposit.

locatio operarum — the hire of service, ie the contract of employment.

locatio operis faciendi — the hire of services, ie a contract to do a particular piece of work.

locatio rei — the hire of a thing.

locator — a lessor.

lockfast place — a place (other than a building) which is secured by a lock (eg a room, drawer, box or car), the key not being in the lock. The opening of a lockfast place is an aggravation of the crime of theft.

loco parentis — in the place of a parent.

loco tutoris — in the place of a tutor. A factor *loco tutoris* may be appointed by the Court of Session where a pupil has no tutor.

locum tenens — a person who acts as substitute or depute for another.

locus — the place.

locus delicti — the place where the delict or crime was committed.

locus poenitentiae — place for repentance: an opportunity for reconsideration, ie the right of a party to resile from a contract which is not yet completed unless he is prevented by *rei interventus* (qv), homologation (qv) or some other personal bar.

locus solutionis — the place of payment or performance of an obligation.

locus standi — a place to stand: the right to be heard by a court or tribunal.

lodge — to deposit pleadings or other documents with the clerk of court.

long roll. *See* **rolls**.

loosing of arrestment — the taking off or removal of an arrestment, eg on finding caution or making consignation (qv).

Lord —
  (1) a title of honour given to a peer of the realm and also as a courtesy title to the sons of
      a duke or the eldest son of an earl;
  (2) a title accorded generally to judges of the Court of Session and, within their own
      courts, to sheriffs;
  (3) a title incorporated in the titles of certain other honourable offices though the
      holders are not necessarily peers, eg the Lord President, the Lord Justice-Clerk, the
      Lord Justice-General, the Lord Advocate, the Lord Lyon and a Lord Provost.

Lord Advocate — the senior law officer of the Crown in Scotland. He is a member of
  the government, advising it on legal matters affecting Scotland, is in charge of the
  prosecution of all crime, and is responsible for the Lord Advocate's Department
  where, among other things, legislation affecting Scotland is drafted.

Lord High Commissioner — the Queen's representative at the General Assembly of
  the Church of Scotland.

Lord Justice-Clerk — the second in rank of the Scottish judges who constitute the
  Court of Session and the High Court of Justiciary. He presides over the Second
  Division of the Inner House of the Court of Session.

Lord Justice-General — the presiding judge of the High Court of Justiciary. In 1823 the
  office was combined with that of Lord President of the Court of Session.

Lord Lyon King-of-Arms — an officer (who takes his title of Lyon from the armorial
  bearings of the kings and queens regnant of Scotland, the lion rampant) who has wide
  jurisdiction in the Court of the Lord Lyon in all heraldic matters and who is responsible
  for the ordering of state ceremonies. His functions correspond to those discharged in
  England by the Earl Marshal and Garter King of Arms.

Lord Ordinary — a Senator of the College of Justice who sits in the Outer House of the
  Court of Session and determines cases there at first instance.

Lord President — the first in rank of the Scottish judges who constitute the Court of
  Session and the High Court of Justiciary. He is the presiding judge of the First Division
  of the Inner House of the Court of Session. *See also* **Lord Justice-General**.

Lord Provost — the chairman of the district council comprising each of the cities of
  Aberdeen, Dundee, Edinburgh and Glasgow.

Lords Commissioners of Justiciary. *See* **High Court of Justiciary**.

Lords of Council and Session — originally members of the king's council in Scotland
  who combined political and judicial functions in the fifteenth century. They are now
  the judges of the Court of Session.

Lords of the Articles — a committee appointed by the Crown to which the Scots
  Parliament delegated most of its powers in the sixteenth century.

lucratus — enriched; frequently relevant in the context of that aspect of unjustified
  enrichment called recompense. A person who has benefited by the work or services of
  another which were not rendered in implement of contract may be obliged to
  remunerate the party who has provided the benefit, not for all that party's expenditure
  but to the extent of benefit enjoyed *quantum lucratus*, ie in so far as he is enriched.

lucrum cessans aut damnum emergens — gain ceasing or damage arising. Either kind of
  loss attracts the liability of the person who caused it.

Lyon Court — the court of the Lord Lyon King-of-Arms (qv).

m

mace — an ornamental staff of authority borne by a macer (qv) before a judge of the
  Court of Session and displayed in his court when the court is sitting.

macer — a mace bearer or usher in the Court of Session. Macers were recognised as
  members of the College of Justice on its formation in 1532, but their functions are less
  important in modern practice than formerly.

magistrate — generally, any person with judicial powers. The term is now applied to provosts and bailies of burghs, as previously constituted, and also to stipendiary magistrates presiding in the district court, but not (as in England) to justices of the peace.

mail *or* **maill** — an obsolete term for rent. Thus blackmail is illegal rent. The action of maills and duties still exists as a form of diligence enabling a heritable creditor to receive payment of rent directly.

majori minus inest or majus includit minus — the greater includes the less. Thus a conveyance of heritage includes not only the land itself but also all the ancillary rights attached to it.

majority — the status of a person of full age (eighteen since 1969 but formerly twenty-one) and capacity. Cf **minor.**

mala fide — in bad faith; lacking good faith.

mala grammatica non vitiat chartam — grammatical error does not vitiate a deed if the meaning is clear and intelligible.

male appretiata — wrongly valued. Confirmation (qv) *ad omissa vel male appretiata* is competent where any estate was originally omitted or undervalued.

malice — the preconceived intention to cause mischief or injury to another. Reckless or culpable disregard for common justice may, as with evidence of personal ill will, be sufficient to constitute malice.

malicious mischief — the crime of maliciously destroying or damaging the property of another.

malitia supplet aetatem — malice supplies the place of age. Formerly the presumption that a child in pupillarity was incapable of forming criminal intent was rebuttable if such intention could be proved.

malum in se — an intrinsic evil; an act which is inherently wicked. Cf *malum prohibitum.*

malum prohibitum — a forbidden evil: an act which is wrongful because it is prohibited, although it is not necessarily morally wrong, eg exceeding the speed limit.

malum regimen — bad or unskilful medical treatment. It may be pled as a defence to a charge of homicide when the victim of an assault dies following defective medical treatment.

malus animus — dole, or evil intention: the state of mind required to make conduct criminal in general or in relation to a particular crime. In English law, and now generally in Scotland, *mens rea.*

malversation — corrupt behaviour in an office of trust.

man of skill — an expert to whom a court may remit a matter before it for investigation and report.

mandant — a person who authorises another to act for him under a contract of mandate (qv).

mandatary. *See* **mandatory.**

mandate —
(1) *mandatum*: a contract whereby a person (the mandatory) is authorised by another (the mandant) to act gratuitously on his behalf, eg a power of attorney;
(2) the actual authority conferred under the contract of mandate.

mandatory *or* **mandatary** —
(1) (n) a person who is authorised to act under a contract of mandate (qv);
(2) (adj) describes a requirement which must be complied with (as contrasted with a merely directory requirement) or a statutory requirement which cannot be altered by a court.

mandatum. See **mandate.**

manse — a dwellinghouse provided for a parish minister.

mansuetae naturae — of a tame nature. *See* *domitae naturae.*

manu aliena — by the hand of another.

manu propria — by one's own hand.

march — a boundary, especially that between one farm or estate and another. The land on the border between Scotland and England was called 'marches'.

mark —
  (1) an old Scots coin: *see* **merk**;
  (2) an old Scots weight;
  (3) a cross or other sign by which deeds were formerly subscribed by those who were blind, but now incompetent as notarial execution (qv) is now provided for those who are thus disabled;
  (4) to enter or give notice of an appeal in a litigation.
marking — a system, abolished in 1933, by which the pursuer in an action raised in the Court of Session could select the Lord Ordinary to hear the cause or the Division of the Inner House to hear it on review.
marriage contract — an ante- or post-nuptial contract which regulates property rights to be enjoyed by the spouses and their issue. The English term 'marriage settlement' is sometimes substituted.
Martinmas — a quarter day in Scotland (11 November), a term day for the payment of rent, although under the Removal Terms (Scotland) Act 1886 entry to and removal from a house agreed to take place at Martinmas take place at noon on 28 November.
master and servant — an obsolescent term for 'employer and employee'.
materiality — the importance or significance of some question, factor or particular which may be at issue in a dispute. For example, in the law of contract a material (ie significant) departure from one of the terms of the contract might entitle a party to resile or recover damages.
matrimonium ipsum — marriage itself. Consent at the time the marriage is constituted is essential to the contract. Consent or agreement to marry in the future does not constitute the contract, although such a promise, if followed by intercourse, might formerly have constituted an irregular marriage.
maxim — a phrase or sentence comprising a short, succinct statement of legal principle, and usually, in Scots law, derived from Roman law and expressed in Latin. It is sometimes called a brocard (qv).
media concludendi — the grounds of action; the basis on which the pursuer seeks a decree.
medio tempore — in the meantime.
meditatio fugae — the intention of absconding. A warrant *in meditatione fugae* by which a debtor intending to abscond abroad might be apprehended and imprisoned was formerly in frequent use but has been incompetent since 1880.
medium filum fluminis — the middle line of a river, which often forms the boundary between properties on opposite banks.
melior est conditio possidentis vel defendentis — the condition of a possessor or of a defender is better. Thus in a dispute the onus is on the challenger or pursuer.
meliorations — improvements to property made by a liferenter or tenant, the costs of which are irrecoverable from the fiar or landlord. Cf **pejorations**.
members' club — a club the assets and property of which belong to the members. *See* **club.**
memorandum of association — a document subscribed by persons seeking the registration of a limited company, setting out the name, capital, objects and powers of the company. Cf **articles of association.**
memorial — a document, usually prepared for counsel by an instructing solicitor, setting out the relevant facts and circumstances and specifying the matters on which counsel's opinion is required.
mens rea — guilty purpose or criminal intent. Cf *actus non facit reum, nisi mens sit rea* and *malus animus.*
mens testatoris in testamentis spectanda est — in the construction of a will the testator's intention is to be regarded. If the words of the will are clear, they will be held to express that intention. If there is doubt, his presumed intention derived from the rest of the will will prevail as a construction.
mercantile law — that branch of the law which is concerned with the legal principles and customs affecting business, commerce and trade.
mercy — the royal prerogative of clemency whereby the sovereign might pardon a convicted offender or reprieve and commute a sentence imposed upon him.

merits — that part of a claim or defence which is concerned with the rights or wrongs or the essence of the dispute or litigation between parties, as distinct from technical or ancillary considerations.

merk *or* **mark** —
(1) an old Scots coin of the value of thirteen shillings and four pence Scots (*see* pound Scots);
(2) a measure in udal law.

messengers-at-arms — officers of court appointed by the Lord Lyon to serve and execute writs and warrants of the Court of Session and the High Court of Justiciary. They are also sheriff officers (qv) and as such discharge similar functions for the sheriff court.

messis sementem sequitur — the crop follows the sowing. The person who in good faith sows crops on land possessed by him is entitled to reap those crops.

metus causa — through fear. Deeds executed or contracts entered into through fear may be reduced.

midcouples — statutes, decrees or deeds used or referred to as links, tracing an entitlement to heritable property, in what is called a deduction of title.

minerals — fossils, fuels and other materials below the surface of heritable property which pass with the conveyance of the heritage or which may be reserved. At common law gold and silver belong to the Crown, and by statute oil is vested in the Crown and coal in British Coal (formerly the National Coal Board).

minor — a person under the age of eighteen; or, more precisely, a person who has ceased to be a pupil (a pupil (qv) being a boy under the age of fourteen or a girl under the age of twelve) but who has not reached the age of eighteen. A minor has legal personality but limited active legal capacity.

minority — the status of a minor (qv). When he reaches the age of eighteen he attains majority (qv).

minority and lesion. *See* **enorm lesion.**

minus solvit qui tardius solvit — he pays too little who pays late: the principle under which interest may be exigible in respect of a debt where due payment is delayed.

minute — a document which forms part of the process (qv) of a civil litigation. In it a party (or both parties jointly) may state a position on some aspect of the case or make a procedural application.

minute book —
(1) a book containing in succinct form particulars of the acts and decrees pronounced by the Court of Session;
(2) a book kept at the office of the General Register of Sasines (qv) containing brief particulars of details of deeds presented for registration.

minute of wakening. *See* **sleep.**

miscarriage of justice — a serious injustice in the course of a criminal trial which usually leads to the conviction being quashed.

misdirection — a mistake in law made by a judge in the course of his charge or directions to the jury.

misfeasance — the wrongful or unlawful performance of official duty: a term of English law often used now in Scotland in relation to company law.

misprision of treason — the crime of simply knowing, without any participation, of treason and failing to report it forthwith to the proper authorities.

misrepresentation — an untrue statement which is successfully designed to induce someone to enter into a contract. It may render the contract void or voidable and, if fraudulent or negligent, may found a claim for damages.

missives — in the sale of heritable property, the probative letters exchanged by the parties which constitute a binding contract and set forth its terms and conditions in detail.

mitigation — alleviation or amelioration. A plea in mitigation normally follows conviction at a criminal trial in an attempt to lessen the severity of the sentence to follow.

mob — a group of persons acting together in riotous violence or intimidation for a common illegal purpose. *See* **mobbing**; **rioting**; **stouthrief**.

mobbing — the crime of participating in a mob (qv).

mobilia sequuntur personam — moveables follow the person. Moveable property is transferred or dealt with (eg in the law of sale or succession) in accordance with the personal law of its proprietor.

modify — to restrict eg expenses or a penalty.

modus — manner or method.

modus habilis — a competent method. *See* *habile modo.*

modus operandi — the method of operation or the manner of doing something.

modus tenedi — the manner of holding, eg the tenure by which land is held.

modus transferendi dominii — the actual form by which the transfer of the ownership of property is expressed and effected, as opposed to *titulus transferendi,* which is merely the will or intention to do so.

moiety — one of two equal parts or shares; more loosely, one of two or three not necessarily equal parts.

moorburn. *See* **muirburn.**

mora — delay.

mora **taciturnity and acquiescence** — a plea in litigation to the effect that delay now bars any entitlement to assert a claim or right.

morte legatarii perit legatum — a legacy lapses on the death of the legatee prior to the testator's death.

morte mandatoris perit mandatum — a mandate (qv) falls on the death of the mandant.

mortgage — an English term for the grant of a loan secured on moveable or immoveable property, commonly now used in Scotland to describe a loan to assist in the purchase of heritable property and secured by a standard security (qv) over the property itself.

mortis causa — in contemplation of death. *See* **donation** *mortis causa.*

motion — an oral or written application to the court in the course of civil or criminal proceedings.

motion roll. *See* **rolls.**

Motor Insurers' Bureau — an institution established by insurance companies in agreement with the Department of Transport to satisfy established claims for damages in respect of losses arising from road traffic accidents which should by statute have been, but were not, insured against.

mournings — the reasonable expenses incurred by a widow on attire etc appropriate for mourning on the death of her husband, constituting a privileged debt, akin to funeral expenses, chargeable against the estate of the deceased.

moveable property; moveables — all property not classed as heritage (qv). Corporeal moveable property, such as furniture, vehicles and animals, can be handled or moved. Moveable property which has a legal but no actual physical existence, such as debts and company shares, is classed as incorporeal moveable property.

muirburn *or* **moorburn** — the burning of heath or moorland (including the heather or grass on it) which is subject to statutory regulation under the Hill Farming Act 1946. The exercise of the right is called 'making muirburn'.

multiplepoinding (pronounced 'multiplepinding') — an action in which the court is asked to adjudicate upon conflicting claims made to property or money (called the 'fund *in medio*') held by a person who is called either the 'real raiser' where he brings the action or the 'nominal raiser' where a claimant brings the action.

multures (pronounced 'mooters') — the proportion of grain formerly required to be given to the miller for grinding it. Dry multures were duties in grain or money paid whether grain was ground or not. *See* **thirlage**.

munus publicum — a public office, such as that of a judge, formerly held *ad vitam aut culpam* (qv), and involving duties to the public.

murder — the crime of homicide committed intentionally or with wicked disregard for the consequences of one's actions.

murmur — to defame a judge, whether in writing or orally, by imputing to him corruption, partiality, oppression or failure of duty in his office.

mutatis mutandis — changing that which has to be changed; making the necessary alterations. Thus a deed or writ which is used as a style in another similar situation will be adapted *mutatis mutandis*, the particulars special to the circumstances being appropriately altered.

mutual gable — a wall between two buildings and forming a gable to each. Each adjacent owner has a right of property in his own share of the wall and both have a common interest in the whole.

mutuum — equal return: a species of loan; a contract under which fungibles (qv) are lent for consumption without payment on the basis that an equal amount of the same commodity will be returned to the lender by an agreed date.

n

narrative — the clause, usually the opening clause, in a deed which sets forth the names and designations of the parties, the consideration and, where appropriate, the circumstances giving rise to the deed.

nasciturus — yet to be born. Rights may be conferred by law or by destination (qv) on those to be born in the future.

natural justice — the equitable principles of fairness governing the conduct of a litigation, arbitration or hearing to determine an application or dispute. These include the principles that no man can be judge in his own cause, that each party is entitled to be heard and that justice be not only done but also be seen to be done.

natural person — a living human individual with legal capacity, rights and duties, as contrasted with a juristic person (qv).

naturalisation — the procedure of conferring nationality or citizenship of a country upon an alien of that country.

nautae, caupones, stabularii. *See* **edict nautae, caupones, stabularii**.

necessitate juris — by necessity of law; necessarily arising from the effect of the law.

negative prescription. *See* **prescription**.

negative servitude. *See* **servitude**.

negligence — failure to exercise a duty required by law to show reasonable care to avoid loss or harm to the person or property of another. Cf **contributory negligence** and **delict**.

negotiable instrument — a document constituting evidence of the right to a sum of money, transferable simply by delivery or indorsement and delivery without the need for a formal transfer, and valid in favour of a transferor's title. Examples include banknotes, cheques (unless marked 'not negotiable'), bills of exchange and promissory notes.

negotiorum gestor — a manager of business; a person who acts with reasonable care but gratuitously and without express authority in an emergency on behalf of another who is unable to act on his own account (eg through absence or incapacity). The *gestor* is entitled to be relieved of liability and expense reasonably incurred.

nemine contradicente — without a dissenter: describes a proposition accepted without contradiction; sometimes abbreviated '*nem con*'.

nemo contra factum suum venire potest — no one can go against his own act; having agreed to a course of action or maintained in pleading a particular position, one cannot do or maintain something different.

nemo dat quod non habet — no one can give what he has not got. One cannot acquire title from a person who is not the owner or his agent.

nemo debet bis vexari — no one ought to be troubled twice; one may not be called upon to answer a second time for the same offence, ie when one has 'tholed an assize' (qv).

nemo debet esse judex in propria causa — a rule of natural justice that no one ought to be judge in his own cause.

nemo debet ex alieno damno lucrari — no one should be enriched out of the loss or damage sustained by another: the principle founding the law of unjust enrichment.

nemo ex proprio dolo consequitur actionem — no one can pursue an action based on his own fraud or wrongdoing. *See* **ex dolo non oritur actio**.

nemo judex in parte sua. *See* **nemo debet esse judex in propria causa**.

nemo patriam in qua natus est exuere nec ligeantiae debitum ejurare possit—no one may abandon his native country or forswear the obligation of allegiance, unless, of course, he becomes a national of another country.

nemo plus juris ad alium transferre potest quam ipse habet — no one can transfer to another a greater right than he has himself. Thus the *bona fide* purchaser of stolen property acquires no better right to it than the thief had.

nemo praesumitur malus — no one is presumed to be bad. This maxim embodies the principle of the presumption of innocence.

nemo tenetur ad impossibilia — no one is bound to perform impossibilities.

next of kin — before 1964, relatives entitled at common law to succeed to moveables on the death of the owner. Strictly a spouse is not next of kin, and an ancestor is not necessarily so. The phrase is also used loosely in other contexts to mean a person's nearest relative or relatives, including a spouse.

nexus — bond, tie, fetter or connection. Thus an arrestment is said to create or attach a *nexus* to the property or fund arrested.

nihil agitur si quid agendum superest *or* **nihil perfectum est dum aliquid restat agendum** — nothing is done, or effectually performed, if anything still remains to be done. The maxim applies where something requires to be done completely before it can be said to be done effectually or at all. Thus the conveyance to the purchaser of heritage must not only be executed and delivered but it must also be recorded if it is to be effective.

nimious — excessive, as in the phrase 'nimious and oppressive'.

no case to answer — a submission which may be made on behalf of the accused at the close of the Crown case in a criminal trial to the effect that there is insufficient evidence in law at that stage to justify a conviction. If the submission is successful, the accused is there and then acquitted of that charge.

nobile officium — noble office or power. The High Court of Justiciary or the Court of Session may use this ultimate equitable power, as distinct from its *officium ordinarium*, within strict limits to modify the rigorous application of the common law or to give proper relief in a situation for which the law has made no provision.

nomen juris — legal term: any word having a particular technical legal meaning, eg 'heritage' and 'sale'.

nomen universitatis — the name of the whole together, a term describing a right which incorporates a variety of different or supplementary rights, eg a barony, which includes title to the land and also other related and subsidiary rights.

nominal raiser. *See* **multiplepoinding**.

nominate contract — a contract possessing a *nomen juris* (qv), such as sale, from which the legal rules and consequences are implied and readily understood. Innominate contracts, by contrast, are unusual agreements creating no rights and obligations other than those expressly agreed between the parties.

nominatim — by name, as when a testator expressly names beneficiaries rather than describing them as a class, eg grandchildren.

non . . . . *See* **nemo . . . .** Some Latin maxims begin with either word.

non bis idem — not the same thing twice. *See* **nemo debet bis vexari**.

non compos mentis — of unsound mind.

non constat— it does not hold; it may or must not be assumed from one fact, admitted or proved, that another fact is true. The phrase refers to unwarranted assumptions of fact. Cf **non sequitur**.

non decipitur qui scit se decepi— he is not deceived who knows that he is being deceived. One cannot plead fraud, deception or misrepresentation in seeking to reduce or avoid the consequences of a contract if one knew all along of the fraud, deception or misrepresentation.

non entia — things having no existence; nonentities. Thus documents which require by law to be stamped may not be looked at by the court.

non exemplis sed legibus judicandum — things are to be judged not by examples but by laws. Thus disputes must be determined on principles of law, not on precedents based on particular instances.

non memini — I do not remember. Where a party to an action to whose oath the case has been referred swears '*non memini*', he is entitled to absolvitor unless what he says that he cannot remember is so recent that he is disbelieved and can, in those circumstances, be said to have confessed.

non obstante — notwithstanding; not opposing.

non officiendi luminibus vel prospectui — of not obstructing the lights or prospects; the servitude of light or prospect, a negative servitude which may be constituted only by express grant.

non remota sed proxima causa spectatur. See causa proxima, et non remota, spectatur.

non sequitur — it does not follow, ie it does not follow from an assumed state of fact or argument that a particular conclusion can be drawn. The phrase refers to an illogical inference. Cf *non constat.*

non utendo — by non-usage. Rights that may be acquired by long usage may similarly be lost by long non-usage. Cf *res merae facultatis.*

non valens agere — not able to act. Prior to 1924 if and whilst a person was not able legally to act by reason of minority or some other disability, prescription did not run against him.

non videntur qui errant consentire — those who are in error are not to be taken to consent. Thus voluntary obligations entered into in essential error may be rescinded.

nonage — the state of not being of full age, ie the state of being in minority (qv) or pupillarity (qv).

not guilty —
(1) a plea by a person accused of a criminal charge whereby he denies his guilt and requires the Crown to attempt to prove the charge at the trial;
(2) a verdict of acquittal in a criminal trial which is appropriate where the judge or jury is satisfied of the innocence of the accused or where the Crown has failed to prove his guilt beyond reasonable doubt.

not proven — an alternative verdict of acquittal in a criminal trial, appropriate where the judge or jury is seriously suspicious but is not satisfied that the accused has been proved to have committed the alleged offence.

notarial execution — a procedure whereby a deed may be subscribed by a notary on behalf of a blind or illiterate person: see the Conveyancing (Scotland) Act 1924, s 18(1).

notarial instrument — any instrument drawn up and executed by a notary; more especially such an instrument, introduced in 1858, used and recorded for the purpose of infeftment where the direct recording of a conveyance itself was inconvenient, insufficient or impossible. It was superseded by the notice of title (qv).

notary public — a solicitor, admitted as a notary public by the Court of Session, before whom affidavits and other documents may be sworn.

note —
(1) an incidental application in the Inner House of the Court of Session or in certain proceedings in the sheriff court;
(2) a statement appended to an interlocutor in sheriff court proceedings setting out the grounds upon which the sheriff has proceeded.

notice of title — an instrument superseding the notarial instrument (qv) setting out the right of a person to heritable property which, when recorded in the General Register of Sasines or the Land Register of Scotland, completes the person's title to the property.

notice to quit — a notice given by either party to a lease intimating an intention to bring the contract to an end.

notour bankruptcy — formerly a state of insolvency which had become 'notorious'. The circumstances in which the state arose were prescribed by statute. It was a prerequisite to the initiation of sequestration proceedings by creditors. It has been replaced by apparent insolvency (qv).

novatio non praesumitur — novation (qv) is not presumed: the new obligation must be shown to replace the old one completely, failing which it may be regarded as corroborative of the old or as constituting a separate and additional obligation.

novation — the extinction of a contractual obligation and its replacement by a new obligation with the consent of all the parties concerned.

novodamus — we give of new: a charter by which a superior renewed a feudal grant of heritable property already made. It was granted in order to enlarge, alter, replace or correct the previous title.

novus actus interveniens — something new intervening: a fresh circumstance which may or may not break the connection between cause and effect or consequence.

nudum pactum — a mere paction; an unenforceable understanding or engagement.

nudus cum nuda in loco suspecto non paternoster dicere praesumuntur — an unclothed man and woman found together in a suspicious place are presumed not to be praying together: a presumption of consistorial law which is difficult to rebut even in modern conditions. *See also* **solus cum sola in loco suspecti**.

nuisance — an act or omission at common law or under statute, usually connected with the occupation of heritable property, which causes annoyance, damage or inconvenience to others and based on the maxim *sic utere tuo ut alienum non laedas* (qv).

nullity — non-existent, lacking legal force etc when used of ineffective acts or writs which are null and void. *See also* **nullity of marriage.**

nullity of marriage — an action for declarator, competent in the Court of Session. The contract of marriage is void when it has, from the start, suffered from an inherent defect such as the existence of a prior marriage, relationship within prohibited degrees or want of consent. Divorce, followed by habit and repute, may cure the first defect. The contract of marriage is voidable on grounds of impotency of either party.

nuncupative — oral, not written, especially of a legacy which, if proved by parole evidence, is valid in the case of moveables to a value of £100 Scots.

nuptias non concubitus sed consensus facit — consent, not cohabitation, constitutes a marriage.

O

OH — Outer House (qv).

oath — a solemn undertaking, with a formal reference to God, that what is asserted is in fact true or what is promised will be performed, used especially of the pledge made by a witness promising to speak the truth in giving evidence. A person without religious belief may solemnly affirm instead of taking an oath.

oath of calumny — an oath formerly required from the pursuer in a divorce action to the effect that his averments were true and that there had been no agreement to advance a false case or withhold a proper defence. The purpose was to prevent collusion.

oath on reference, *or* **reference to oath** — a form of proceeding, derived from Canon law and competent only in civil causes, under which a litigant is entitled to require his opponent to answer an oath as to the truth of his case or some specific part of it. In certain circumstances and in the absence of relevant writings by his opponent, such a reference may be the litigant's only recourse. The answer cannot be challenged or contradicted, and the person referring is bound by it.

ob contingentiam — on account of connection or similarity. *See* **contingency**.

ob majorem cautelam — for greater security or caution (qv).

ob non solutum canonem — on account of unpaid canon or feuduty. A ground of forfeiture in feudal tenure.

ob pias causas — on account of religious reasons or natural or dutiful considerations.

obediential — of an obligation or duty imposed by law on moral rather than contractual or delictual grounds. Used especially of family obligations.

obiter dictum — an incidental pronouncement; an opinion expressed by a judge, in giving judgment, on a point which is not essential to the decision. Cf *ratio decidendi*.

obligant — the debtor or obligor in an obligation; the person who is liable to perform what has to be done. The creditor is the obligee.

obligation — a legal connection or relationship between two persons arising from unilateral promise, agreement, by force of law or by order of a court, whereby an obligee is endowed with enforceable rights and duties. The law of obligations, based primarily upon Roman concepts, forms a substantial branch of the modern law of Scotland. Its main divisions include obligations arising from unilateral promise, from contract, from delict, from rules to avoid unjust enrichment, from fiduciary relationships, from therequirements of statute and from the judgments of courts.

obligationes literis — a contract which must be constituted in writing, eg one for the sale of heritable property.

obligee, obligor — *See* **obligant**.

obtemper — to obey, comply with or fulfil, used especially of a court order.

occupancy *(occupatio)* *or* **occupation** —
(1) the physical possession and use of heritable property;
(2) the acquisition, with a view to appropriation, of things which have no owner, eg catching salmon or finding pearls.

occupier's liability — the duty of care required of the occupier of premises to those coming on to the premises. It is regulated by the Occupier's Liability (Scotland) Act 1960, which abolished the conceptual categories of invitee, licensee and trespasser introduced from England and applied to Scots law by the House of Lords in 1929.

odal tenure. *See* **udal tenure**. Etymologically 'odal' is the more correct form, but 'udal' has been accepted generally by Scots lawyers and jurists and by custom.

offence — an act or omission which is contrary to and punishable by the law. Acts and omissions prohibited by statute are generally termed 'offences', those offending against common law being called 'crimes'.

offensive weapon — an article made or adapted or carried with the intention of using it for the purpose of causing injury to the person: see the Prevention of Crime Act 1953, s 1.

officium nemini debet esse damnosum — an office should inflict damage upon no one. Thus nobody should incur loss in the discharge of an office or duty. A tutor, curator, mandatory and *negotiorum gestor* (qv) are all entitled to recover expenses reasonably incurred by them.

ombudsman — the colloquial designation, derived from Scandinavian sources, of the Parliamentary Commissioner for Administration, the Commissioner for Local Administration in Scotland and the Health Service Commissioner for Scotland (qv) who, in their respective spheres, investigate complaints of bureaucratic maladministration, ineptitude or injustice.

omissa (vel male appretiata) — items which have been omitted from (or undervalued in) the inventory of the estate of the deceased in the confirmation of an executor. An additional confirmation *ad omissa (vel male appretiata)* or an eik (qv) to the original confirmation may require to be obtained.

omne majus continet in se minus — the greater includes the lesser.

omne verbum de ore fideli cadit in debitum — every word sincerely spoken will constitute an obligation: a rule of Canon law adopted by Scots law whereby verbal undertakings or promises given in earnest can constitute enforceable obligations.

omni exceptione major — beyond all exception, as of a witness whose status or character renders his evidence unimpeachable.

omnia praesumuntur contra spoliatorem — all things are presumed against a wrongdoer. The maxim has no application in criminal law but arises in civil litigation. Thus if one party hides or destroys a document the terms of which are in dispute, it will be presumed to have been in the terms alleged by the other party or, at least, in terms disadvantageous to the loser or destroyer.

omnia praesumuntur rite et solemniter acta esse (or omnia rite acta praesumuntur) — all things are presumed to have been solemnly done and with the usual ceremony: the rebuttable presumption of compliance with the appropriate formalities.

omnis definitio in jure periculosa est — all definition in law is dangerous. For a judge to define or limit the meaning or application of the law too nicely is dangerous, because he cannot foresee all the circumstances or cases to which the law may be applied and the inconvenience and injustice which might ensue.

omnis ratihabitio retrotrahitur et mandato priori aequiparatur — every ratification operates retrospectively and is equivalent to a prior authority. To ratify or homologate what has been done without authority has the same effect as if the act had been authorised at the time of its performance, in other words the homologation has retrospective effect.

onera realia — real burdens; encumbrances affecting heritable property.

oneris ferendi — bearing a weight or burden: an urban servitude by which the dominant proprietor may rest the weight of his building on the wall or property of the servient proprietor.

onerous — given for value, payment or services, as opposed to gratuitous.

onus of proof (*onus probandi*) — the burden of proving each disputed issue of fact arising in a litigation. This rests upon one party or the other. If that burden is not discharged by the party on whom it rests, he usually fails on that issue. Procedural considerations and sometimes statute regulate the incidence of burden of proof, but it generally rests on the prosecutor or pursuer on the principle that he who asserts something must prove it.

ope et consilio — by aid and counsel; aiding and abetting; art and part.

ope exceptionis — by force of exception (qv); a plea by way of peremptory and preliminary objection in a civil cause that a document which is founded on, and which concerns the parties to the cause alone, should be set aside as null and void. It is particularly useful in the sheriff court where the alternative action of reduction is not competent.

open record — a document comprising the written pleadings of the parties to a civil action, prepared at a stage when the pleadings are incomplete and capable of adjustment. Cf **closed record**.

opinion —
   (1) counsel's written expression of his views on the law applicable in a particular set of circumstances presented to him for that purpose (*see* **memorial**);
   (2) a statement by a judge of the Court of Session or the House of Lords setting forth the reasons for his judgment.

opinion evidence — a form of evidence given by an expert and constituting his views, arising from his knowledge and experience, on some aspect of a litigation.

oppression — vindictiveness or disregard of the essentials of justice, formerly a ground of appeal against sentence in summary criminal proceedings.

opus manufactum — artificial work, eg earthworks to prevent flooding, in contrast with what is natural.

Order in Council — an order made by the Queen in session with her Privy Council, either by virtue of the royal prerogative or under statutory authority. Orders in Council are generally issued in the statutory instruments series.

ordinary cause or action — any civil proceedings in the sheriff court, other than a summary cause or proceedings for which a special procedure is provided. Ordinary causes are regulated by the Ordinary Cause Rules.

ostensible — describes that which is apparent or seems to be so. Thus an agent may have ostensible authority, creating the impression that he has power to do something when in fact he may not have that power.

Outer House — that part of the Court of Session in which Lords Ordinary, sitting alone, try cases at first instance, so-called because the court was originally situated closer to the courthouse entrance than the Inner House (qv).

outwith — outside; beyond; away from.

overriding interest — a temporary or permanent restriction or other right over heritable property (eg a lease or servitude) which binds the proprietor whether or not it is recorded in the General Register of Sasines or registered in the Land Register of Scotland. See the Land Registration (Scotland) Act 1979, s 28(1).

overrule — to reverse or correct the decision of an inferior court in the same or in separate and later proceedings.

oversman — an umpire upon whom a decision in an arbitration is to devolve where the arbiters fail to reach agreement.

overt — open; public; not concealed.

P

PC —
  (1) Privy Council;
  (2) Privy Counsellor;
  (3) police constable.

pacta dant legem contractui — the stipulations of the parties constitute the law of the contract. These stipulations may differ from the common law or statute, but will be enforced if not illegal or immoral.

paction — an agreement or bargain.

pactum — a bargain, agreement or paction.

pactum de non petendo — an agreement not to seek; an agreement, absolute or temporary, not to require performance of an obligation.

pactum de quota litis — an agreement for a share of the subject of a law suit. Such an agreement by a lawyer for a 'contingency fee', ie to accept a share of what may be recovered by legal action in place of a fee, is illegal and void in Scotland but is permitted in certain foreign jurisdictions.

pactum de retrovendendo — an agreement to sell back. The most common modern example is an agreement that a seller of heritable property is to have a right of pre-emption upon any resale.

pactum donationis — an agreement to give in donation. It creates a *jus ad rem* or personal obligation on which the donee may sue the donor for performance or for damages for breach of the agreement.

pactum illicitum — an illegal contract or agreement.

panel, pannel — a person appearing in court upon an indictment charged with a crime or offence.

par in parem non habet imperium — an equal has no power over an equal. Thus a judge is not bound to follow or regard as a precedent the decision of another judge of equal jurisdiction and, conversely, the one has no power to review or alter the decision of the other.

paraphernalia — an obsolete term for a woman's personal possessions, including her clothes and jewellery, which remained her property notwithstanding marriage and never became her husband's property.

pari passu — in equal grade; equally, as of a right to share equally with others a common fund in multiplepoinding (qv), sequestration (qv) and the like.

Parliament House — the building in Edinburgh comprising the Court of Session, the High Court of Justiciary and their attendant offices. It also contains the hall where the Parliament of Scotland sat until the Union of 1707.

Parliamentary Commissioner for Administration — an officer, popularly called the 'ombudsman', who investigates complaints of injustice arising from alleged maladministration by government departments.

parole —
(1) the conditional release of a prisoner before he had served his full sentence;
(2) spoken, as opposed to written.

parole evidence — oral evidence given *viva voce* by witnesses, as distinct from real or documentary evidence.

parricide — the murder of a parent by his or her child.

pars contractus — part of the contract. If it is agreed that a contract should be reduced to writing, that agreement being *pars contractus*, the contract does not become binding until that is done.

pars judicis — the part or duty of the judge; that which a judge must notice and act upon, irrespective of the wishes of the parties, eg his duty to dismiss proceedings which it is not competent for him to determine.

parte inaudita — one party being unheard, as of an *ex parte* (qv) application in court, eg for interim interdict, or a decree pronounced *in absentia*.

particeps criminis — partner in crime; accomplice.

particeps fraudis — partner in fraud.

partner — a person carrying on a business in common with another or others with a view to profit.

partnership —
(1) the contractual relationship between persons carrying on a business in common with a view to profit;
(2) a firm comprising partners.

parts and pertinents — everything which passes with the actual land on its transfer or disposition, eg minerals, servitudes and fishing rights.

partus sequitur ventrem — the offspring follows the mother — a rule of natural accession whereby the young of animals belong to the owner of the mother at the time of their birth.

passing off — an actionable wrong comprising the misrepresentation of a business or goods with the purpose or effect of misleading the public into thinking that the business or the goods are those of another.

pasturage — a servitude entitling the dominant proprietor to graze his cattle, sheep and horses on the servient tenement.

patent — a monopoly right over an invention granted for a specified period by the Crown. Patents are now regulated by the Patents Act 1977.

pater est quem nuptiae demonstrant — he is the father whom the marriage indicates to be so. Thus children born to a married woman are rebuttably presumed to have been fathered by her husband.

patria potestas — paternal power; the power which a parent has as guardian of a child.

patrial — a person having the right to live in the United Kingdom.

patrimonial — pertaining to inherited estate or property.

patrimonial loss — strictly, loss sustained by one's estate, now a term of art in reparation claims for the loss of money or any property which can be assessed in monetary terms, as distinct from pain and suffering arising from physical injury or injury to feelings.

patrimony — an estate or property inherited from an ancestor.

pawn — to deliver an article of moveable property to another as security for a debt or other obligation. Cf **pledge**. At common law 'pawn' and 'pledge' were synonymous.

pejorations — deteriorations to heritable property made by a liferenter or tenant. This term is occasionally used in contradistinction to meliorations (qv).

penal — of punishment; attracting punishment as a penalty; punitive.

penal damages — punitive or exemplary damages. Such damages by way of reparation are not recoverable in Scotland.

pendente lite — during the dependence of a litigation; so long as an action is pending before the court.

pendicle — a small piece of land, subsidiary to a larger estate, or something attached to another thing. In older conveyancing practice the phrase 'parts, pendicles and pertinents' was sometimes used. *See* **parts and pertinents.**

penuria testium — scarcity of witnesses. Formerly this justified calling as witnesses those otherwise disqualified because of relationship or interest.

per aversionem — by bulk or aggregate quantity, as of the sale of a particular un-quantified crop or cellarful of wine.

per capita — by heads. In succession, where an estate is to be divided among beneficiaries (eg grandchildren) *per capita*, it is divided equally among them, and the right of representation (eg of their parents) *per stirpes* (qv) is excluded. A charge *per capita* (eg the community charge) is one based on the actual number of people liable to pay it.

per curiam — by the whole court; a term of English law referring to a dictum expressed unanimously by judges participating in a decision.

per incuriam — through mistake or error, describing eg a judgment delivered in ignorance of a decisive precedent or statutory provision.

per modum exceptionis — by way of exception: a defence admitting the relevancy of a claim, but denying the conclusion on grounds eg of force or fear.

per se — by itself or by himself or herself.

per stirpes — according to the roots. In succession, where the estate is to be divided among beneficiaries *per stirpes*, it is not just the survivors who benefit; the share of a predeceasing beneficiary is divided among his children. Cf *per capita*.

per subsequens matrimonium — by subsequent marriage. Children born out of wedlock are legitimated by their parents' subsequent marriage.

perceptio — a gathering in. A person in possession of land in good faith who gathers in the fruits of that land thereby becomes their owner. If the land really belongs to another, ungathered fruits *(fructus pendentes)* remain the property of the true owner.

peremptory — admitting no denial, absolutely fixed, as of a diet (qv) at which the case must proceed.

perficere susceptum munus — to perform the duties of an office undertaken. Anyone who undertakes an office or duty must perform the obligations thereby incumbent upon him and, until he has done so, he may not capriciously resign.

periculo petentis — at the risk of the petitioner. All judicial warrants obtained *ex parte* (qv) are granted at this risk. Thus if the operation of an interim interdict, obtained groundlessly, causes loss, the petitioner will be liable in damages.

periculum rei venditae nondum traditae est emptoris — the risk of a subject sold, but not yet delivered, lies with the purchaser. This rule of the common law was an exception to the general rule *res perit suo domino* (qv). Since the Sale of Goods Act 1893, s 20 (now the Sale of Goods Act 1979, s 20), the risk normally transfers to the buyer when the 'property' in the goods passes, whether or not the goods have been delivered.

perinde est ac si scriptum non esset — it is the same as if it had not been written. When the words of a deed fail to convey its meaning, extrinsic evidence will not be admitted to prove what the granter intended, and the deed will be void for uncertainty.

periodical allowance — a regular alimentary payment fixed by the court and payable by one spouse to another following their divorce.

perjury — a common law crime committed by a person who, under oath or affirmation, wilfully gives evidence in judicial proceedings which he knows to be untrue.

permanent trustee — an insolvency practitioner (qv) elected by the creditors or appointed by the court to administer a sequestration (qv). Cf **interim trustee**.

personal bar — the rule precluding a person from maintaining that which he has previously denied.

personal bond — a written undertaking, without security, to pay a debt or perform an obligation.

personal estate, personal property or personalty — English terms for moveable property.

personal right. *See jus in personam.*

personation — pretending to be somebody else. Personation of a policeman, or of a voter at an election, is criminal under statute. If fraudulently undertaken, personation is criminal at common law.

pertinents. *See* **parts and pertinents**.

perverse verdict —
(1) a verdict where the jury has deliberately declined to obey the judge's direction on a matter of law;
(2) loosely, a verdict which, in the judge's opinion, flies in the face of common sense.

perverting the course of justice — a common phrase used in formal charges to describe the purport of a number of common law crimes involving interference with witnesses, fabrication of evidence, escaping from custody and the like.

pessimi exempli — of the worst example; affording a very bad precedent. To allow someone to benefit under a contract induced by his fraud would be *pessimi exempli*.

petition —
(1) a primary application to the court seeking authority to enable the petitioner to do some act which would otherwise be unauthorised or asking the court to order another to do some act which the petitioner cannot himself require that person to do: such an application forms one branch of the principal classification of causes in the Court of Session, the other being the summons (qv) (the classification does not exist in the sheriff court);
(2) loosely, an application to a court;
(3) to present a petition to the court.

petition and complaint — an application to the Court of Session, made with the concurrence of the Lord Advocate, for the exercise of the court's criminal or quasi-criminal jurisdiction. In the Inner House such an application is appropriate for malversation, misconduct or neglect of duty by a judicial officer, and in the Outer House for breach of interdict.

petitioner — a person who presents a petition to the court.

petitory action — an action in which the court is asked to order the defender to do something to fulfil an obligation to the pursuer, eg to pay a debt.

pignus — a pledge; the contract of pledge.

plagium — the crime of stealing a human being. In modern practice it is restricted to child stealing.

plea in bar of trial — a plea in criminal proceedings that the trial cannot proceed for want of jurisdiction or because the accused is insane.

plea in mitigation — a plea made to the judge before sentence by or on behalf of a convicted person seeking to show cause why a lenient sentence should be imposed.

plea of irrelevancy — a defence that an action is not relevant (qv).

plead —
(1) to present and argue a case in court;
(2) to present a case in writing.

pleadings — the formal written presentation of his case in court by a party to a civil action.

pleas in law — concise legal propositions with which the pursuer and the defender in civil proceedings conclude their written pleadings and upon which they found their respective cases. There are pleas in law directed to the merits of the case and preliminary pleas raising issues which require to be disposed of before the merits are considered.

pleas of the Crown — the crimes of murder, robbery, rape and wilful firevaising, all formerly capital offences reserved to the High Court of Justiciary. The concept now has no practical significance.

pled — pleaded.

pledge —
(1) an item of moveable property delivered as security for an obligation, usually a debt;
(2) the contract (*pignus*) constituted by delivery of such property;
(3) to deliver moveable property as a pledge.
Cf **pawn**. At common law 'pledge' and 'pawn' were synonymous.

plenishing — furniture, equipment, stock or gear; moveable property brought on or into heritable property, especially to furnish it.

pleno jure — with full right. The transfer of property *pleno jure* carries the property with all the profits or advantages pertaining to it.

plenum dominium — the full right of property, including both the *dominium directum* and the *dominium utile* (qv).

pluris petitio — a claim for more than is due. Such a claim may affect expenses. To seek a larger random sum of damages than that which is ultimately awarded is not *pluris petitio*.

plus enim valet quod agitur, quam quod simulare concipitur — that which is done is of more avail than that which is pretended to be done. The law will have regard to the real character of a transaction rather than the form in which it was effected. Thus a debtor is entitled to insist upon a reconveyance of property conveyed by an *ex facie* absolute disposition when it was truly granted in security.

plus petendo tempore — where a creditor sues for a debt prematurely, he is seeking it *plus petendo tempore*. He renders himself liable to pay the expenses of defending his claim.

plus quam tolerabile — more than can reasonably be endured. The phrase is used eg:
  (1) as of extraordinary damage to crops or temporary partial damage to subjects let which might entitle a tenant to some abatement of rent, or
  (2) to describe the degree of interference with rights of property (eg noise) which constitute an actionable nuisance.

poaching — the crime of taking game or fish without legal right or authority.

poind (pronounced 'pind') — to impound a debtor's corporeal moveables in his own hands in execution of diligence as a preliminary to their public sale or adjudgment to the creditor in satisfaction of a decree.

poinding schedule — a document prepared by the court officer executing a poinding, identifying the creditor and the debtor, listing the articles poinded and their respective values and stating the sum recoverable and the place where the poinding was executed.

poinding the ground — a form of diligence available to heritable creditors whereby moveables on the land over which the debt is secured are impounded as a preliminary to their public sale in satisfaction of the creditor's decree.

police —
  (1) the body of officers responsible for the enforcement of law and order in a particular defined area;
  (2) an obsolete term for the civil domestic administration of the country, though it was more usually applied to the internal regulations for watching, lighting, cleaning and punishing minor delinquencies in great cities.

policies — enclosed grounds of a substantial residence; park.

policy of insurance — an instrument constituting a contract of assurance.

pondere, numero et mensura — by weight, number and measure. The tests apply to ascertain whether goods are fungibles (qv).

poor's roll — the roll of litigants who, by reason of poverty and having *probabilis causa litigandi* (qv), were formerly entitled to sue or defend *in forma pauperis* (qv). The legal profession provided counsel and solicitors who were prepared to act in such circumstances without fee. The roll has now been superseded by the provision of legal aid in civil and criminal causes.

Porteous Clerk — an officer who formerly travelled from place to place to hear evidence of crimes.

Porteous Roll — a list of offenders' names and file of indictments in early criminal procedure.

portio legitima — legal portion; legitim (qv).

positive prescription. *See* **prescription.**

positive servitude. *See* servitude.

posse comitatus — the power or force of the county; the police or officers of court whom the sheriff has a right to require to assist in the enforcement of court orders.

possessio bona fide — possession in good faith in the belief that the possessor is entitled to possession and knows of no other person with a better right. Such possession carries the right to the fruits of the property which the possessor has gathered.

possessio mala fide — possession in bad faith, in the belief that another is the true proprietor. A person possessing property in bad faith is liable to that other person for all the fruits of the property and for violent profits (qv).

possession — physically holding or retaining a corporeal moveable or physically occupying heritable property with the intention of keeping it as one's own property or for one's own use.

possessory action — an action (eg for interdict or removing) to retain or recover possession of property which another has wrongfully claimed or acquired.

post hoc ergo propter hoc — after this therefore because of this: illogically ascribing the cause of a result to an event simply because the event preceded the result.

post litem motam — after an action has been raised. The subject of a pending litigation cannot effectively be altered to the detriment of either party.

post tantum temporis — after so long a time.

posteriora derogant prioribus — later enactments repeal earlier ones. Even if it is not expressly stated therein (though it usually is), a provision in an Act of Parliament inconsistent with or opposed to a provision in an earlier Act operates to repeal it.

postponed debt — a debt which is payable in a sequestration only after all other claims have been satisfied, eg a loan made by the debtor's spouse or partner.

potior est conditio possidentis vel defendentis — the condition of a possessor is stronger. *See* ***melior est conditio possidentis vel defendentis.***

pound Scots — the unit of Scots currency in general use in Scotland before and for some time after the Union of 1707. Its value was one-twelfth of a pound sterling; thus one pound Scots was worth one shilling and eightpence sterling (in decimal currency 8.5p). The pound Scots was divided into twenty shillings Scots, each of which was divided into twelve pence Scots. Six pence were one bawbee. See also **merk**.

power of appointment (*or* **apportionment**) — an authority conferred by deed or will to a person to distribute or divide the property of the grantor or testator, usually in accordance with general guidelines prescribed in the deed or will.

power of attorney — a deed conferring authority granted by one person to another (called the 'attorney' or 'factor') to act on his behalf. Originally a term of English law, it is now widely used in Scotland instead of the Scots term 'factory and commission'.

practicks — collections of notes on decisions of the Court of Session formerly compiled by members of the court (eg Balfour). They were the precursers of the law reports, and were originally recorded chronologically. The later practicks were arranged under subjects as digests.

praeceptio haereditatis — taking an inheritance in advance. To avoid the possibility of an heir otherwise entitled to succeed receiving his inheritance from the testator gratuitously before the testator died, thus avoiding responsibility for the testator's debts, the law describes the heir's title to the property as a 'passive' title incurring liability for the debts unless the heir can prove that the transfer was onerous.

praecipuum — taken before others — that part of a testator's estate which is not subject to division and so formerly passed to the eldest of heirs-portioners, eg titles of honour and the mansion house of the estate.

praedial — affecting land, especially of servitudes.

praedium — land; heritable property.

praepositura — the power conferred by a principal upon an agent or servant to execute the principal's business and thereby bind him; the presumption that a wife was placed by her husband in charge of the household, so that he was liable for contracts entered into by her within the scope of her ostensible authority. That presumption was abolished in 1984. Ordinary principles of agency are now considered to suffice.

praepositus negotiis — entrusted with the charge of certain affairs, ie vested with the *praepositura* (qv). The principal is liable for obligations thus incurred.

praepositus negotiis societatis — placed over the affairs of business of the partnership. The contract of partnership implies that each party is entrusted with the partnership business and may thus bind the firm.

praescriptio longissimi temporis — the prescription of the longest period. The period of forty years during which certain rights were either acquired or extinguished was reduced to twenty in 1973.

***praeses* *or* preses** — the elected chairman of a meeting, especially a meeting of creditors.

praesumendum est pro libertate — the presumption is in favour of liberty. There is such a presumption against any restrictions upon the full and unrestrained enjoyment of property, and servitudes are thus strictly construed.

praesumitur pro legitimatione — the presumption is in favour of legitimacy. Thus all children born in wedlock are presumed to be the children of the spouses.

praesumptio hominis vel judicis — the presumption of the man or judge, the judge's opinion arising from the circumstances of the particular case laid before him.

praesumptio juris — a legal presumption which may be rebutted. Thus ownership of moveables is presumed from possession, and debtors are presumed not to make gifts to creditors.

praesumptio juris et de jure — a legal presumption amounting to a legal rule, which may not be rebutted.

praesumptione — by presumption; according to the *praesumptio juris* (qv).

precarium — a form of the contract of *commodatum* (qv) where the subject is lent not for a particular time or occasion but indefinitely, and is returnable at the will of the lender.

precatory — praying; describes words in a will which pray or express the desire that a thing be done, without positively directing it. Whether their effect is precatory or mandatory is a question of construction.

precedent —
(1) a court decision regarded as authoritative in deciding later cases;
(2) an English term for a style or model form of a legal document used as a pattern or in drafting other documents.
See also **condition**.

precept — a warrant or order.

precognition — a preliminary written statement of the evidence which a witness may be expected to give. It is usually paraphrased after interview with the witness and prepared in the first person. It is not signed, and is not binding.

pre-emption — a right to buy before another has the opportunity to do so.

preferred debt — a debt which is payable on bankruptcy or the winding-up of a company in preference to other debts (eg taxes, social security contributions and employees' wages).

preliminary plea — a plea in law (qv) by either party in a civil action that is purely technical and does not go to the merits but which, if sustained, results in the dismissal of the action or its defence. Examples are pleas that the pursuer has no title to sue, that the court has no jurisdiction to hear the case, that the action is incompetent or that the pleadings for the pursuer or the defender are irrelevant.

prerogative —
(1) the common law royal superiority of the Sovereign involving powers, privileges and dignities most of which are now subject to the authority of Parliament (the prerogative of mercy is now exercised in Scotland upon the advice of the Secretary of State);
(2) a right or dignity attached to an office.

presbytery —
(1) a court of the Church of Scotland comprising ministers and elders largely from congregations within the presbytery (as defined in (2)), the functions of which include superintending kirk sessions within the presbytery and electing members to the General Assembly of the Church of Scotland;
(2) the area which is under the jurisdiction of a presbytery (as defined in (1)), the numbers and boundaries of such areas being designated by the General Assembly.

prescription — rules of law by which certain rights and obligations are established or extinguished or the modes of proving them are limited by lapse of time; the legal inference of:

(1) the grant of a right arising from long usage and enjoyment of the right (positive prescription: 10 years, or 20 years in certain cases), or

(2) the extinction of a right arising from abandonment or long neglect to exercise or enforce the right (negative prescription: 5 years, or 20 years in certain cases).

The rules are now regulated by the Prescription and Limitation (Scotland) Acts 1973 to 1984.

presents — the use of the words 'these presents' within a document means the document itself.

preses — the elected chairman of a meeting, particularly a meeting of creditors.

prestable — capable of being executed or enforced; payable; exigible.

prestation — what requires to be done under an obligation or duty.

presumption — an inference as to the existence of one fact drawn from the admission or proof of the existence of another fact. The inference may amount to a legal conclusion, rebuttable or otherwise, arising by law from a given set of facts. Alternatively it may be a practical conclusion inferred from the facts held to be proved.

presumption of death — the presumption under the Presumption of Death (Scotland) Act 1977 that a person who has disappeared and either is thought to be dead, or has not been known to be alive for more than seven years, is dead. A declarator to that effect may be sought from the court.

presumption of innocence — a fundamental rule of criminal law that a person charged with a crime or offence is presumed to be innocent unless and until he is proved at a trial and beyond reasonable doubt to be guilty. The onus of proving the charge therefore remains upon the Crown, as prosecutor, throughout the trial.

presumption of life — the presumption at common law that a person known to have been alive at a particular time continues to be alive for a reasonable period thereafter, probably at least eight years.

pretium affectionis — the price of regard; sentimental value; the value of a thing due to the owner's regard for it, irrespective of intrinsic value, as with heirlooms, gifts from deceased relatives etc.

pretium periculi — the price of the risk; an insurance premium.

prevarication — concealment or misrepresentation of the truth by giving evasive or equivocating evidence. It is usually demonstrated by a witness avoiding giving proper answers to legitimate questions, and is punishable summarily as a contempt of court.

prima facie — at first appearance or sight. A *prima facie* case is one which, at first sight, appears compelling and calls for an answer.

primo loco — in the first place. *Secundo loco* means in the second place, and so forth.

primo venienti — to the person who comes first; first come, first served. If six months after a death the estate of the deceased appears solvent, the executor must pay all creditors known to him, and if any others appear while the estate is still undistributed then he will pay *primo venienti*.

primogeniture — first born. The former rule that the eldest male descendant was entitled to succeed to the heritable property of an intestate parent as heir at law. It is now obsolete except in respect of transmissible titles, honours and dignities.

Prince and Great Steward of Scotland — one of the titles of the eldest living son of the Sovereign.

principal — a person for whom another acts, or purports to act, under a contract of mandate or agency (qv).

Principality of Scotland — the lands of the Stewartry of Scotland and certain other lands constituting an apanage of the Prince of Scotland (qv).

prior rights — rights of the surviving spouse of a person dying intestate to the dwellinghouse, with furniture and plenishings, and financial provision out of the estate. The rights rank after those of creditors but before those of all other beneficiaries.

prior tempore potior jure — prior in date, preferable in right. Thus in a competition the conveyance first recorded gives a preferable right to one recorded subsequently, irrespective of the dates of the actual conveyances.

prison breaking — the crime of escaping or attempting to escape from local custody in prison.

private Act of Parliament — a local or personal statute which grants special powers or rights to an individual, a local authority, a public corporation or a limited company. If solely applicable to Scotland the procedure is usually regulated by the Private Legislation Procedure (Scotland) Act 1936.

privative jurisdiction — jurisdiction exclusive to a particular court.

privilege — the legal right in particular circumstances to do or not to do something free from normal restriction. Thus it may afford a defence to an action for defamation. Privileged statements in such cases may be either absolute (eg statements in Parliament or in judicial proceedings) or qualified (where the statement was made under a duty to someone with an interest to receive it). In the latter case the defence fails if malice is proved. Privilege in evidence may allow a witness to withhold from disclosure certain communications (eg between a party and his legal advisers).

privileged debts — debts owed by the estate of a deceased person (eg expenses of confirmation, funeral and deathbed expenses, mourning and taxes), which are payable before debts of unsecured creditors.

Privy Council — the principal council of the Sovereign. It exercises a judicial function in certain appeals through the Judicial Committee of the Privy Council (qv).

pro bono publico — for the public good; for the advantage of the public generally.

pro confesso — as having confessed. Thus a person is generally held *pro confesso*, ie to have admitted a claim, if he does not appear to answer or defend a civil action raised against him.

pro forma — as a matter of form; as of proceedings which are purely formal or a partly printed formal document which requires completion by insertion of particulars.

pro hac vice — for this turn; for this occassion, as of an appointment to an office or duty to effect one particular task.

pro indiviso — in common; in an undivided manner; as of one person's right in property owned in common by two or more persons.

pro loco et tempore — for the place and time. Thus a prosecutor may desert criminal proceedings *pro loco et tempore*, while reserving the right to renew the prosecution at a later date.

pro non scripto — as not written; matters in a deed that are ignored, eg illegal or impossible conditions in a will.

pro possessore habetur qui dolo desiit possidere — he is held to be the possessor who, for a fraudulent purpose, has ceased to possess. All the liabilities of a possessor must be borne by such a person.

pro privato commodo — for private convenience. Contrast *pro bono publico*.

pro rata — proportionately. Joint debtors or creditors are only bound by or entitled to the shares of the debt due *pro rata*. Joint and several debtors are each indebted to the creditor *in solidum* but only *pro rata* in a question with each other.

pro re nata — in an emergency; out of the ordinary course, as of a meeting or proceedings necessarily called or taken to consider or meet a sudden emergency.

pro tanto — for so much; to account of. When a defender consigns a sum admitted but the pursuer obtains decree for the whole sum claimed, the pursuer may uplift the amount consigned and apply it *pro tanto* in satisfaction of his decree.

pro tempore — for the time being; temporary.

pro veritate — as if true.

probabilis causa litigandi — a probable or plausible ground of action. Thus an applicant for legal aid must demonstrate that he has a reasonable case for taking or defending the proceedings in question.

probate — the certificate, granted by the High Court in England, that a will has been proved, constituting the title of the executors to the testator's estate and evidence of their right to administer it.

probatio probata — a proved proof. Where there is no provision for an appeal on the facts (as distinct from matters of law), the facts found to be established by a jury or by a judge at first instance may not be contradicted.

probation —
(1) proof in civil proceedings (*see also* **conjunct probation or proof**);

(2) a requirement imposed by order on a person found guilty of a crime or offence that he submit, subject to conditions, to the supervision of a social worker for a specified period (the order constitutes a final disposal of the criminal proceedings but does not constitute a conviction).

probatis extremis praesumuntur media — the extremes being proved, what falls within or between them is presumed.

probative — self-proving, as of a deed which, when executed in accordance with the prescribed formalities (eg as to subscription and attestation), itself constitutes proof that it is authentic and is unchallengeable except in proceedings for its reduction.

procedure roll. *See* **rolls.**

process —
(1) all the formal collected documents and papers relating to a civil action;
(2) a civil action.

process caption — a summary warrant to imprison a person who has removed or borrowed a process from the court and failed to return it.

procuration — agency, commonly applied to agency to sign a bill of exchange.

pro-curator — a person who has acted as curator without having been legally appointed as such.

procurator —
(1) a solicitor practising in the sheriff court or the district court;
(2) an advocate appointed as official legal adviser to the General Assembly of the Church of Scotland.

procurator fiscal — an officer appointed as his agent by the Lord Advocate to act within a sheriffdom as public prosecutor in the sheriff court and the district court, to investigate and report serious crime to the Crown Office, to investigate sudden or suspicious deaths and to initiate fatal accident inquiries.

procuratorio nomine. See proprio nomine.

procuratory — an authority, mandate or commission to a person to act for another.

production — a document or article produced as evidence in court (in English law called an exhibit).

progress of titles — the series of successive and linking recorded sasine title deeds, extending over at least ten years, which, prior to registration under the Land Registration (Scotland) Act 1979, constitutes evidence of a secure title to heritable property.

prohibition notice — a notice served by a health and safety inspector prohibiting activities which the inspector considers will involve risk of serious personal injury. Cf **improvement notice.**

promissory note — an unconditional promise to pay money made in writing by one person to another, eg a cheque.

proof —
(1) the formal hearing of evidence in a civil case by a judge sitting at first instance;
(2) the establishment of a fact by evidence;
(3) loosely, evidence itself;
(4) in England, a written statement by a witness of his evidence in a case.

proof before answer — the formal hearing of evidence as to the facts before the court decides the questions of law raised by a preliminary plea (qv).

proof in replication — the hearing of evidence which, with leave, may be led by the pursuer after the defender has completed his evidence, if some unforeseen matter has come to light.

propone — to put forward, submit or propound.

proprietary club. *See* **club.**

proprietor — the person having a right to property (usually heritable property), even though his title is not complete.

proprio jure — by one's own proper right.

proprio nomine — in one's own name. When one sues for oneself, one sues in one's own name and character. If a trustee or a factor or the like sues in that capacity, he sues *procuratorio nomine.*

propter commodum curiae — for the advantage of the court.

propter eminentiam masculini sexus — on account of the superiority of the male sex: a justification which, with its feminine counterpart *propter fragilitatem sexus* (on account of the weakness of their sex), formerly explained privileges extended respectively to men or to women. They must now be regarded as discredited.

propter fragilitatem sexus. *See* **propter eminentiam masculini sexus.**

prorogate —
  (1) to confer on a court, by consent of the parties, jurisdiction to hear a case by waiving objections to it;
  (2) to extend a time limit, as of a procedural order in the course of a litigation.

prosecution — a litigation in which the Lord Advocate or the procurator fiscal on his behalf institutes and pursues a criminal charge before a court. In bringing a prosecution the Lord Advocate, procurators fiscal and their deputes enjoy absolute privilege.

protest — a procedure for establishing proof of dishonour of a bill of exchange or promissory note, whereby a notary public presents or 'protests' the bill or note to the drawer or acceptor for payment, failing which the notary 'notes' the date and fact of the dishonour on the bill or note and declares the fact in a certificate or 'protest'. Once registered in the Books of Council and Session or the Sheriff Court Books the protest may be extracted and diligence can proceed.

protestation — a procedure by which the defender in a civil action compels a pursuer who has not lodged his summons for calling in the Court of Session or tabled his case in the sheriff court in due time either to proceed with or abandon his action.

protocol —
  (1) an original;
  (2) a record of a diplomatic transaction;
  (3) an entry in a protocol book kept by a notary recording an instrument or act.

pro-tutor — a person who has acted as tutor without having been legally appointed as such.

prout de jure — according to law. A general proof according to law is thus called in contrast to a proof restricted to the writ or oath of a party.

proving the tenor — an action in which the pursuer seeks, by proving from drafts, copies or otherwise the contents of a lost or destroyed document, to replace it by a decree to the same effect.

provisio hominis non tollit provisionem legis — a provision made by an individual does not abrogate the provisions of the law. Thus no one by will or settlement can circumvent legal rights.

provisional order — an order issued by the Secretary of State at the request of its promoters as part of the preliminary procedure for the enactment of a private Act of Parliament (qv).

provocation — words or actions which have the effect of exciting or inspiring the commission of a crime of violence. If proved it may have the effect of reducing murder to culpable homicide. It is not otherwise a defence but may be a mitigating factor in the assessment of the appropriate sentence.

Provost — the chief magistrate and chairman of a town or burgh council prior to 1975. The title is now held by the chairmen of some district councils. *See also* **Lord Provost.**

proximate cause — in delict, the closest effect or factor causing loss or harm. *See* **causa proxima, et non remota, spectatur.**

proxy —
  (1) a person appointed to vote for and in the absence of another person at an election or meeting, eg a shareholders' meeting;
  (2) a document appointing such a person.

puberes — minors (qv).

public analyst — an analyst appointed by a local authority under the food and drugs legislation to act as analyst for its area.

public burdens — public taxes and assessments imposed in respect of the ownership or occupation of heritable property.

public general Act — a statute of general application, as contrasted with a private Act of Parliament (qv).

public roup — a public auction.

punctum temporis — point of time.

pupil — a boy under the age of fourteen or a girl under the age of twelve. A pupil has passive legal capacity to acquire rights but is incapable of acting or consenting in legal transactions. A tutor acts or consents for a pupil. Cf **minor**.

pupillarity — the status of a pupil.

pure; **purify** — obligations are either *pure* or *in diem*. Performance of the former can be required at once, because there are no conditions attached to them. Performance of the latter can only be insisted upon when that day arrives, ie when the conditions have been fulfilled or 'purified'.

purge an irritancy — to clear an irritancy (qv) by remedying the default which led to it before decree or declarator that the irritancy exists is granted. Legal but not conventional irritancies may be purged.

pursuer — a person instituting or suing in a civil action (in English, a plaintiff).

putative — believed; reputed, as of the alleged father of an illegitimate child.

q

QC — Queen's Counsel (qv).

qua — as; in the character of; eg when a person sues not in his own individual interest but *qua* trustee.

quadriennium utile — the period of four years following the attainment of majority, during which the reduction of any transaction may be sought on grounds of minority and lesion. *See* **enorm lesion**.

quae ab initio non valent ex post facto convalescere non possunt — that which was invalid from the beginning cannot be made better by a subsequent act. Thus a contract which is fundamentally null and void or a procedure which is fundamentally incompetent cannot be corrected by some later act.

quae perimunt causam — taking away the ground of action; used of defences or pleas which take away the ground of action; a successful defence on the merits which leads to absolvitor and constitutes *res judicata* of the issues between the parties.

quaere or quaeritur — it is questioned; the question is raised.

qualified privilege. *See* **privilege**.

qualify — to establish by evidence; to authenticate.

quamprimum — as soon as possible; forthwith.

quando aliquid mandatur, mandatur et omne per quod pervenitur ad illud — when anything is ordered to be done, everything is ordered by which the performance of the order may be accomplished. Thus a decree, competently pronounced by a judge, automatically carries with it the power to enforce that decree by diligence.

quando aliquid prohibetur, prohibetur et omne quod devenitur ad illud — when anything is forbidden, everything which amounts to the forbidden thing is also forbidden. This is the counterpart of the preceding maxim. It is most often found in patent cases where the patent right is infringed under the colour or pretext that something else is being used than that which has been patented. Further, an agreement between a creditor and a bankrupt may be struck at if, in truth, it is really a device to effect a fraudulent preference.

quando res non valet ut ago, valeat quantum valere potes — when a thing is not valid as I do it, it may still be valid to some extent. Thus if a bill of exchange or promissory note is, for want of some particular, invalid for summary diligence, it may still be excellent evidence to support an action for payment.

quanti minoris — for how much the less. *See* **actio quanti minoris**.

quantum — how much; the extent of the damages payable; thus in a reparation action it is necessary first to establish liability and then to determine *quantum*.

quantum lucratus — as much as he has been enriched, as of gain or profit in an action based on recompense rather than on contract. Cf **quantum meruit**.

quantum meruit — as much as he has earned. Thus where services have been rendered or work has been performed without prior contractual agreement as to the amount to be paid for it, an action will lie for payment *quantum meruit*, a fair remuneration.

quantum valeat — as much as it is worth; for what it is worth. Evidence the competency or relevancy of which is doubtful may be admitted for subsequent consideration *quantum valeat*.

quarter days — Candlemas, Lammas, Martinmas and Whitsunday.

quasi — as if; as though.

quasi-contract — an obligation to avoid unjust enrichment created by force of law and not by contract, such as recompense, restitution and *negotiorum gestio*.

quasi-delict — a confusing term, perhaps best used for cases of strict liability to make reparation irrespective of intention or negligence (eg liability under the praetorian edict *nautae, caupones, stabularii* (qv)).

Queen's and Lord Treasurer's Remembrancer — the holder of two Exchequer offices who now combines a number of miscellaneous responsibilities including the collection of fines and penalties, auditing the accounts of sheriff clerks and procurators fiscal, and more exotic activities such as administering treasure trove and caring for the Regalia of Scotland.

Queen's Counsel — a senior and experienced member of the Faculty of Advocates (or of the English Bar), appointed as such as an honour by the Sovereign. Upon appointment the Queen's Counsel 'takes silk', his entitlement to wear a silk gown.

quem nuptiae demonstrant — whom the marriage indicates or points out. *See* **pater est quem nuptiae demonstrant.**

quh . . . — in early Scots, equivalent to 'wh', eg quha, who; quhare, where; quharever, wherever; quhat, what; quhatsumever, whatsoever; quhen, when; quhile or quhill, while; quhilk, which; quhilom, formerly; quhose, whose.

qui alterius jure utitur eodem jure uti debet — he who exercises the right of another ought to exercise the same right. Thus rights exercised by an agent can never be greater in extent or character or used differently from those which the principal could exercise himself.

qui approbat non reprobat — one who approbates may not reprobate. Thus a person may not take advantage of a benefit conferred upon him by one part of a deed or contract and disregard or dispute another portion which may impose some unwelcome condition on the benefit.

qui facit per alium facit per se — he who acts by another acts himself: the principle of vicarious liability. Thus an employer is liable in delict for the consequences of his employee's negligence in the course of carrying out his duties, and a principal is liable for his agent's actions done on his behalf.

qui haeret in litera haeret in cortice — who holds by the letter holds by the bark. Thus the law looks to the substance of deeds to ascertain the parties' intentions, not just the 'skin deep' words which might cloak intention.

qui in utero est, pro jam nato habetur, quoties de ejus commodo quaeritur — in any question which may arise touching its rights or interests, a child in the womb is held as already born. Thus if a right vests whilst a child is *in utero*, the child, after its birth, is entitled to the rights of a living person from the date of its conception.

qui jure suo utitur nemini facit injuriam — he who asserts his own right does wrong to no one. Thus a proprietor is entitled to build right up to the boundary of his neighbour's property.

qui non negat fatetur — he who does not deny, admits: an important rule of written pleadings. If an opportunity to answer has been given, a statement that is not denied is held to have been admitted.

qui potest et debet vetare, jubet si non vetat — he who can and ought to forbid, orders if he does not forbid. Thus if an officer unjustifiably orders his ordinary soldiers to fire upon a crowd, the soldiers, who are bound by obedience, may be excused, but if a superior officer is standing by and hears the order being given and does nothing about it, he is just as responsible for the order as if he had given it himself. Cf ***qui tacet consentire videtur.***

qui suum recipit licet a non debitore, non tenetur restituere — he who receives that which is due to him, although it be not from his debtor, is not liable in repetition or restitution (qv). When a payment is made under the mistaken belief that it is due, repetition can be required under the *condictio indebiti*. Where, however, the friend of the debtor pays off the debt for him and later he is unable to get reimbursement from the debtor, he cannot then insist on repetition on the basis that he was not the true debtor in the obligation.

qui tacet consentire videtur — he who does not object is held as consenting; silence imposes consent. Where a party to an action knows it has been conducted in his name and takes no step to disclaim it, he is held by his silence to have authorised it. Cf ***qui potest et debet vetare, jubet si non vetat.***

qui totum dicit nihil excipit — he who says everything, excepts nothing. Thus a general disposition of his estate by a testator carries the whole estate; it cannot be maintained that some particular thing, of which no mention is made, is excepted.

quid juratum est — what has been sworn; that which has been deponed to. In a formal reference to the oath of a party, the truth of what the party says under oath is not a matter for decision. The only question is what the party has actually said under oath.

quid juris? — what is the law?

quid pro quo — something, usually of similar or equal value, given in return for something else; the price paid for goods.

quid valet nunc — what it is now worth.

quilibet est rei suae arbiter — everyone is the judge of his own affairs; one may do what one pleases with one's own.

quilibet juri pro se introducto renunciare potest — a person may renounce a right which exists solely for his own use or benefit.

quinquennial prescription — the five-year prescription (qv).

quisque scire debet cum quo contrahit — everyone ought to know with whom he contracts. Some obligations are not binding because of the position or character of the person granting them, notwithstanding the *bona fides* of the grantee. Thus an obligation entered into by a minor without the consent of his curator may be reduced even if the other party was unaware of the minority. Likewise, a good title can never be acquired in respect of stolen goods, even by an innocent purchaser.

quo animo? — with what intention?

quoad . . . — as regards . . .

quoad fiscum — as regards the rights of the Crown.

quoad omnia — as regards all matters.

quoad potest — in so far as one is able; to the extent of one's powers.

quoad sacra — as regards sacred things.

quoad ultra — as regards the rest. In pleadings in civil actions part of the pursuer's statement may be admitted and *quoad ultra* there may be a denial.

quoad valet seipsum — as regards its real value; so far as it is worth.

quoad valorem — as regards the value; to the extent of the value.

quocunque — in whatever way; in any way.

quod ab initio non valet in tractu temporis non convalescit — that which is invalid from the beginning does not become more valid by the lapse of time.

quod constat curiae operae testium non indigit — what is clear to the court does not need the aid of witnesses: the principle of judicial knowledge.

quod fieri debet facile praesumitur — that which ought to be done is easily presumed. Thus where something is done as required by law, it is presumed to have been done properly. If a deed appears to have been executed in accordance with the due formalities, it is presumed that the witnesses were present and saw the granter subscribe or heard him duly acknowledge his signature.

quod non apparet non est — that which does not appear, does not exist. Thus if some thing is not produced or some fact is not proved, the court will not regard it as existing.

quod nullius est fit domini regis — that which is the property of no one becomes the property of the Sovereign. Thus, subject to statutory exceptions, heritage that falls vacant reverts to the Crown and moveable property abandoned by its owner belongs to the Crown.

quod nullius est fit occupantis — that which is the property of no one becomes the property of the person finding it or taking possession of it. Thus moveable property (such as game) which has never had an owner becomes the property of the hunter who takes it. The fact that the property had never had an owner distinguishes this maxim from the previous maxim.

quomodo constat? — how does it appear? How is it shown?

quomodo desiit possidere — in what way he lost possession. When claiming possession of a lost moveable subject it is necessary to show previous possession and how it came to be lost.

quorum — of whom; in the context of members of a body attending a meeting, the minimum number of members who must be present to constitute a valid meeting. The word is singular, not plural.

quorum usus consistit in abusu — the use of which consists in consuming them. Thus fungibles (qv) perish in being used.

quota — a share or proportion.

quovis tempore — at whatever time; at any time.

r

R — Regina, the Queen, or Rex, the King.

rack rent — the maximum rent obtainable for a heritable property, based on its full annual value.

raise —
(1) to draw up eg a document;
(2) to institute or bring legal proceedings.

ranking sale — an obsolete judicial procedure whereby the heritable property of an insolvent person was sold and the proceeds divided among his creditors.

rape — the crime of having sexual intercourse with a female against her will.

ratio decidendi — the reason of the decision; the principle of law justifying and underlying the decision of a court; the ground on which a case is decided.

ratio scientiae — the reason of knowledge. The grounds on which a witness's knowledge of the facts of which he has given evidence is based is his *ratio scientiae*. If it is hearsay (qv), that evidence may be valueless.

ratione — by reason; on account of.

ratione contractus — because of the contract.

ratione delicti — because of the delict.

ratione originis — because of one's origins.

ratione rei sitae — because of the position or situation of the property.

re infecta — the thing not having been done; performance having failed.

real burden — an obligation or encumbrance which is attached to and is a charge on heritable property as well as the person of the debtor.

real evidence — any thing (including a human being) tendered as evidence, as distinct from written or spoken evidence.

real raiser. *See* **multiplepoinding.**

real right (*jus in re*) — a right enforceable against all. Contrast *jus ad rem* (qv).

real warrandice. *See* **warrandice.**

rebus integris — matters being complete or intact. Where nothing has been done following a purported agreement or contract, then, the matter being intact and neither party having altered his position, it may be permissible to resile without penalty, eg where there was a verbal agreement to sell heritage but no missives or conveyance followed. Where there has been *rei interventus* (qv), then *res non est integra* and the parties may not resile. Cf *res non est integra.*

rebus sic stantibus — matters so standing; in the existing state of things.

rebut — to counter an opponent's case with evidence or argument.

recall — to bring back; to revoke.

receiver — an individual, who must be an insolvency practitioner (qv), appointed by the holder of a floating charge (qv) or the court to control and manage a limited company in the place of its directors in the interests of the holder of the floating charge and other creditors and the company itself.

reclaim — to submit an interlocutor pronounced by a Lord Ordinary in the Outer House of the Court of Session or by the vacation judge to the Inner House for review, ie to appeal.

reclaiming motion — a motion by which a party reclaims (qv). Formerly the procedure was by reclaiming note.

recompense — an obligation of unjustified enrichment to restore value to a person from whose lawful act, done without intention of donation or contractual obligation, another has gained and the first person has lost. Thus *bona fide* expenditure improving the value of property in the mistaken belief that one owns it may entitle one to recompense from the actual owner.

reconvention — the rule of jurisdiction which enables a person to counterclaim or bring a cross-claim against another who, although otherwise beyond the jurisdiction of the court, has voluntarily submitted himself to its jurisdiction by bringing the principal action there.

record —
  (1) a document forming part of the process (qv) of a civil action and comprising the written pleadings of the parties (the record remains 'open' until, when finally adjusted, it becomes a closed record by order of the court);
  (2) to enter or 'record' a document in an official record such as the General Register of Sasines or the Land Register of Scotland;
  (3) the list of a person's criminal convictions.

Red Mass — a solemn Mass of the Holy Spirit celebrated at the outset of the judicial year and attended principally by judges, sheriffs, counsel and solicitors who are Roman catholics.

reddendo — by handing over; the clause in a feu charter fomerly indicating the obligation to pay feuduty. The creation of new feuduties was abolished in 1974.

redeemable — subject to a right of redemption. Thus the holder of a heritable security has only a redeemable right in the property, whereas a proprietor has an absolute irredeemable right to it.

reduce — to set aside or annul, usually by an action of reduction, a deed, contract, decree or award. *See* **improbation.**

reduction. *See* **reduce.**

redundancy payment — compensation payable under statute by an employer to an employee who is dismissed because his job has ceased to exist through contraction, mechanisation, reorganisation etc.

re-engagement order — an order made by an industrial tribunal requiring the employer of an employee who has been unfairly dismissed to re-engage him in employment comparable to that from which he was dismissed, or other suitable employment. Cf **reinstatement order.**

re-examination — the further examination, subject to certain restrictions, of a witness in court by the party who called him, following cross-examination by another party.

reference to oath. *See* **oath on reference.**

regalia — royal rights; rights of the Crown.

regalia majora — royal rights of the Sovereign which are personal or pertain to the Crown as guardian of the public interest and consequently inalienable without parliamentary sanction, eg rights of navigation over the sea between the foreshore and the offshore territorial limits and navigable rivers, and such prerogatives as the exercise of clemency to criminals.

regalia minora — royal proprietary rights which the Crown may exercise as it pleases and which it may alienate, eg salmon fishings, mines, forests and highways.

Regiam Majestatem — 'The Auld Lawes and Constitutions of Scotland', being an early manual of laws and practice dating from the fourteenth century, first printed in 1609 as edited by Sir John Skene. Some jurists have doubts as to the authenticity of some of the early material.

region — one of the nine areas into which mainland Scotland is divided for local government purposes, each of which is divided into districts (qv). The local authority is the regional council.

Register of Inhibitions and Adjudications — a register kept by the Keeper of the Registers of Scotland in which are recorded inhibitions, adjudications, reductions and notices of litigiosity. Recording in the register is a prerequisite to certain proceedings and actions.

Register of Insolvencies — a public register maintained by the Accountant in Bankruptcy, containing details of sequestrated estates and protected trust deeds.

register of sasines — a public register in which all deeds affecting rights and interests in heritable property required to be recorded for effect. The former particular registers of sasines were abolished in 1868, leaving the General Register of Sasines (qv), which is being progressively superseded by the Land Register of Scotland (qv).

registration for execution — the registration of a deed in the Books of Council and Session or the Sheriff Court Books, which *ipso facto* endows it, for enforcement purposes, with the character of a court decree.

registration for preservation — the registration of a deed in the Books of Council and Session or the Sheriff Court Books in order to preserve it and to enable copies or extracts, the equivalent of the original, to be made.

registration for publication — the registration or recording of a deed relating to heritable property in the General Register of Sasines, thus formally publishing it and *ipso facto* giving effect to it at that date. Cf **registration of title.**

registration of title — registration of a deed relating to land in the Land Register of Scotland, which is gradually superseding the General Register of Sasines. Registration has the effect of vesting in the person registered as entitled a real right in the land ranked according to the date of registration, the right being guaranteed by the state.

rei depositae proprietas apud deponentem manet, sed et possessio — the right of property in a thing deposited remains with the depositor, as does the right of possession. Thus the property in silver left in a bank's safe, or luggage deposited in a left luggage office, does not pass from the person leaving it. The maxim does not apply to fungibles such as cash deposited at a bank.

rei interitus — the destruction of a thing or its ceasing to exist. Performance may not be enforceable if property referred to in a contract is physically destroyed or, for the purposes of the contract, ceases to exist.

rei interventus — the intervention of a thing or act. When one party, to the knowledge of the other, acts to his disadvantage on the faith of an imperfectly concluded agreement, both parties may be bound by the contract.

rei vindicatio — a claim for a thing; the claim by an owner for delivery of a thing against the possessor for the time being.

reinstatement order — an order made by an industrial tribunal requiring an employer to treat an employee who has been unfairly dismissed in all respects as if he had not been dismissed. Cf **re-engagement order.**

reipublicae interest ut sit finis litium — it is in the public interest that there should be a known termination of litigation after which further appeal becomes impossible, or the raising of claims is barred by lapse of time.

relevancy; relevant —
  (1) the pertinence of evidence to a fact in issue in a litigation is a matter of relevancy;
  (2) the relevancy of a claim in civil litigation or a charge in criminal procedure to the remedy sought or its defence or prosecution may be the subject of debate before evidence is heard, and if the pleadings fail to support the case being made or lack appropriate specification, dismissal of that case may follow.

relict — widow or widower. *See jus relictae.*

relocation — *See* **tacit relocation.**

remand —
  (1) the committal of an accused person, in custody or on bail, upon the adjournment of criminal proceedings;
  (2) to commit a person in those circumstances.

remissio injuriae — forgiveness of the offence; condonation as a defence in an action of divorce founded on adultery.

remission *ob contingentiam. See* **contingency.**

remit —
  (1) to refer a case or some portion of it to another court or judge or to an official, either absolutely or for some particular purpose (eg remit to the Court of Session, to the sheriff, to an arbiter, to a man of skill or to the Auditor of Court);
  (2) to extinguish, modify or reduce a sentence or penalty.

removing —
  (1) the relinquishment of possession of heritable property by a tenant, either voluntarily (as by agreement or on breach of contract by the landlord) or compulsorily (which may be either ordinary removing (at the natural ish (qv)) or extraordinary removing (during the currency of the tenancy, through some default on the part of the tenant));
  (2) an action by a landlord to displace a tenant in possession.

rent — the return, usually in money but sometimes in produce or other moveables, due by a tenant or hirer for the possession and use of the property which is the subject of the lease or hire.

rentaller — kindly tenant (qv).

renvoi — a difficulty under private international law where a question of law before a court, for determination according to the law of another country, is remitted there but is remitted back for determination according to the *lex fori* (qv) or, indeed, is remitted elsewhere.

reparation —
  (1) compensation for a delict or civil wrong;
  (2) that branch of the law concerned with delict.

repeal —
  (1) calling back; the revocation of a statutory provision by further legislation;
  (2) to revoke.

repel — to reject or overrule.

repetition — the repayment of money which has been erroneously paid.

replication — reply. *See* **proof in replication.**

repone — to restore a defender against whom a decree has been pronounced in his absence and allow him to defend the case. The process is known as 'reponing', and the application is made by a reponing note. A similar procedure exists in the Inner House of the Court of Session to enable an appeal to proceed where it has been deemed to have been abandoned by some default.

reporter —
  (1) a person appointed to hold a public hearing or inquiry and to report;
  (2) a professional person or other man of skill to whom a court remits a question for advice or investigation and report;
  (3) a person appointed under the Social Work (Scotland) Act 1968 by a regional or islands council to investigate matters concerning children, to arrange and present cases to children's hearings (qv), and for related purposes;
  (4) a person who compiles and edits reports of court decisions for publication.

representation —
(1) a statement made by a person to influence another to enter into a contract with that person (inaccuracy in the statement may entitle the other person to rescind the contract);
(2) in the law of succession, the right of the children of a beneficiary predeceasing the deceased person to succeed to their parent's share.

representative — a person who represents or takes the place of another person.

reprobate — reject. *See* **approbate and reprobate.**

repudiate — to demonstrate by words or conduct that one does not intend to perform one's obligations under a contract.

requisition —
(1) a demand by a creditor for the payment of a debt or the performance of an obligation;
(2) to require, by authority, that the use of something be surrendered.

res accessoria sequitur rem principalem — an accessory follows the principal. *See accessorium principale sequitur.*

res aliena — property or some thing belonging to another.

res communes — common things; things incapable, by their nature, of being appropriated, eg light, air and running water.

res furtiva — stolen property, the right to which remains in the original owner, even if it has since passed to others acquiring it in good faith.

res gestae — things done; the facts and circumstances immediately surrounding or related to a matter at issue in a litigation and of which evidence, otherwise inadmissible, may be allowed.

res inter alios acta aliis non nocet — a thing done between certain people does not injure others. Thus dealings between two parties are generally irrelevant in a question involving different or other parties. Exceptions may occur where there a *jus quaesitum tertio* (qv).

res ipsa loquitur — the thing speaks for itself. Thus the proof of the occurrence of an event may raise a rebuttable presumption of liability in delict.

res judicata — a case or matter decided. Thus a final judgment so disposes of an issue that it may not be raised again in a litigation between the same parties.

res merae facultatis — a matter of mere power; a right the exercise of which depends on the pleasure of the party entitled. Unlike a servitude, such a right cannot be lost by prescription.

res mercatoria. See in re mercatoria.

res non est integra — the matter is not complete or intact. Cf *rebus integris.*

res noviter veniens ad notitiam — things newly come to light, which may warrant the admission of further evidence or even a new trial.

res nullius — something which belongs to nobody. *See* **quod nullius est fit domini regis** and **quod nullius est fit occupantis.**

res perit suo domino — a thing perishes to its owner. Thus, unless the loss is caused by another's fault, loss following destruction or deterioriation is borne by the owner of the property.

res publicae — a thing belonging to the public or the Crown on its behalf, eg a highway, the sea or a navigable river.

res religiosae — sacred things. Churches, communion plate etc are outwith the stream of commerce so long as they are dedicated to religious uses, but the principle is modified in modern practice by statute. See the Church of Scotland (Property and Endowments) Amendment Act 1933.

res sua — one's own property.

res sua nemini servit — an owner cannot have a servitude over his own property. A servitude, being a minor right, can merge with the paramount right of property. Thus, if the owner of the servient tenement acquires the dominant tenement, the servitude may be extinguished.

res universitatis — property belonging to a corporate body, contrasted with the property of an individual.

resale price maintenance — the control of the price at which the purchaser of goods may resell them to a third person.

rescind — to terminate or cancel a contract. A right to rescind arises where the other party wrongly induced the contract, has repudiated it or has committed a material breach of it.

rescission — the termination or cancellation of a contract which has been rescinded.

reservatio ut et protestatio non facit jus sed tuetur — reservation and protest do not make a right, but protect it. Thus the reservation of a right in a deed does not give the right to the granter; he had the right already. The reservation merely preserves or protects if for him.

reservation — a clause in a deed in which the granter of the deed keeps or reserves something for himself.

reset —
  (1) to receive stolen goods knowing them to have been obtained by theft, fraud, robbery or embezzlement, and with the intention of keeping them from their owner;
  (2) the crime of so receiving such goods.

residuary beneficiary *or* **legatee** — a person entitled under a will to the residue of the testator's estate after the payment of debts and expenses and the disposition of specific legacies.

resignation —
  (1) the giving up of an appointment or office;
  (2) formerly, the form by which a vassal returned his interest in land to the superior, permanently (*ad remanentiam*) or for transfer to another, such as a purchaser (*ad favorem*).

resolutive condition — a condition which terminates a right or obligation if a certain specified event occurs.

resoluto jure dantis, resolvitur jus accipientis — the right of the giver having ceased or become void, the right of the receiver also ceases. Thus if a liferenter assigns the benefit of a liferent, the right of the assignee ends on the liferenter's death.

respondeat superior — let the master answer, or be responsible, for the civil wrongs of his employee in the ordinary course of his employment.

respondent — the party in a civil appeal who, whether he was pursuer or defender in the court of first instance, defends the decision against which the appeal has been made.

resting-owing —
  (1) the state of an unpaid bill;
  (2) unpaid.

restitutio in integrum — entire restoration; the restoration of a person to the position in which he would have been had the transaction or event in question not taken place.

restitution — the obligation under unjustified enrichment to restore to the owner property which has been lost and found, delivered by mistake, stolen etc.

resumption — taking back; especially repossession by the landlord of part of the subjects of a lease where permitted by the terms of the lease.

retenta possessione — possession being retained. A pledge of moveables is ineffective without physical delivery to the pledgee.

retention —
  (1) the withholding by one party to a contract of performance of his obligations under the contract until the other party performs his obligations under it;
  (2) more particularly, retaining moveable property until a debt due by its owner is paid, ie a lien.

retentis. *See* **in retentis.**

retro — backward. Some events or acts are said to operate *retro*, ie with retrospective or retroactive effect.

retrocession — reconveyance to the former owner of property or a right conveyed by him to another; often applied to the reconveyance, upon repayment of a debt, of an insurance policy assigned in security.

return day — the date by which the pursuer in a summary cause in the sheriff court must return the summons and certificate of citation to the sheriff clerk. The date is stated in the summons. Cf **calling day**.

reus — the defender, sometimes called *alterior*, contrasting with *actor*, the pursuer.

reverser. *See* **wadset.**

reversion —
(1) in relation to heritage, a right of redemption which may be legal, as in adjudication (qv) for debt, or conventional, as usually set forth in the terms of a heritable security;
(2) the right of the fiar to heritage at the end of a liferent (qv).

reversionary interest — the interest in heritage of the person entitled to exercise a reversion (qv).

review — the reconsideration of a judicial decision on appeal.

revoke — to recall something done earlier, eg a statute, an order of court, the authority of an agent or a will.

rider —
(1) a person with a riding interest (qv);
(2) an addendum or qualification added by a jury to its verdict (thus a verdict of guilty of a charge of assault may be qualified by a rider that the accused had been provoked).

riding interest — the claimed interest of a creditor of a claimant in a multiplepoinding (qv) in the share of the fund *in medio* to which the claimant is or will be ranked.

right of way — the right of a person, either as an individual (in the case of a right of way constituted by servitude) or as a member of the public (in the case of a public right of way), to pass by a specified or recognised route over the land of another. It may be subject to conditions and limitations specified in any grant of the right.

rioting — a crime which, with mobbing (qv), is constituted by the formation of a mob (qv) for a purpose to be accomplished by illegal means such as violence or intimidation to the alarm of the public.

riparian — of or relating to the bank of a river.

riparian owner — the owner of land on the bank of a river.

risk — the possibility of loss or damage. An important question in the contract of sale is the determination of the time at which the risk passes from the seller to the buyer. In matters of insurance it is the risk which is covered by the policy.

robbery — the crime of theft by means of the threat or use of personal violence.

roll of advisings. *See* **rolls.**

roll of defenders — a list of defenders which, where there are more than three, must be lodged with the summons in a civil action in the Court of Session.

roll of proofs, jury trials and special hearings. *See* **rolls.**

roll of undefended causes. *See* **rolls.**

rolls — lists of civil cases set down for hearing in the Court of Session or the sheriff court. The Court of Session rolls, which are published daily during session, include:
(1) the adjustment roll — a list of Outer House cases on which defences have been lodged by the defenders and copies of the open record have been lodged by the pursuer, and which are consequently ready for a Lord Ordinary to close the record;
(2) the calling list — a list of summonses lodged for calling in the Outer House, providing public intimation of actions which have been raised;
(3) the judgment roll — a list of Outer House cases taken to avizandum in which a Lord Ordinary is to give judgment;
(4) the long roll — a list of Inner House cases which cannot yet be heard;
(5) the motion roll — a list of motions entered in the motion sheet in the Outer House;
(6) the procedure roll — a list of preliminary pleas in the Outer House;
(7) the roll of advisings — a list of dates on which judgment will be given in the Inner House in particular cases;

(8) the roll of proofs, jury trials and special hearings — a list of causes in which proofs, jury trials or special hearings have been fixed;

(9) the roll of undefended causes — a list of Outer House causes in which the defenders have failed to enter an appearance or lodge a defence;

(10) the short roll ('the roll') — a list of cases for hearing in the Inner House which are not accorded priority in hearing dates;

(11) the single bill roll — a list of motions etc to be heard in chambers in the Inner House;

(12) the summar roll — a list of cases for hearing in the Inner House which are accorded priority in hearing dates;

(13) the summary trial roll — a list of cases proceeding by summary procedure under the Court of Session Act 1988, s 26.

roup — auction.

royal assent — the approval by the sovereign of a Bill which has been passed by Parliament. Upon receiving the royal assent the Bill becomes an Act and, subject to the provisions of the Act, will thereupon come into force.

rubric —

(1) the long title of a statute, formerly written or printed in red;

(2) the headnote of a reported case.

rules of court — rules prescribing the procedure to be followed in civil causes in the Court of Session (see the Rules of the Court of Session) and the sheriff court (see the Ordinary Cause Rules and the Summary Cause Rules). They are prescribed under statutory powers in the form of Acts of Sederunt by the Lords of Council and Session with the advice of Rules Councils.

rundale land — agricultural land of which intermixed patches or ridges were formerly owned by different persons.

runrig (*or* **runridge**) **land** — agricultural land of which alternate or successive patches or ridges were formerly owned by different persons.

S

SI — statutory instruments (qv).

SR & O — statutory rules and orders (qv).

sale — a contract comprising the transfer by agreement of the ownership of property in consideration of a price.

sale or return — a form of contract of sale by which the goods are delivered to the buyer but the property in them does not pass to him until they are approved and retained. They may otherwise be returned to the seller within a reasonable period.

salus populi* (*or* *reipublicae*) *suprema lex — the welfare of the people (or the state) is the highest law. Thus private interest must always give place to the public welfare. For example, a private house may lawfully be destroyed to check a fire which might otherwise spread throughout a town, and in wartime private interests must give way to the interests of the state in defending the country.

salva substantia — the substance being saved, ie not diminished, as when a liferenter is entitled to the fruits but not the capital or fee of the liferent property.

salvage — a reward, payable under maritime law or under contract, for saving or preserving an endangered vessel or its cargo. The principle has now been extended to aircraft.

salvo jure cujuslibet — reserving the right of all others. The last Act of the sessions of Scots Parliaments was usually so entitled, so as to secure the rights of others against the effects of private Acts. As a saving clause it also formerly appeared in charters of confirmation.

sanae mentis — of sound mind.

sanction — a reward or penalty for observation or contravention respectively of a rule of law.

sasine — an act formerly symbolising the legal acquisition of heritable property. It originally involved a token physical transfer but latterly it comprised registration of the conveyance, or of a notice of title, in the General Register of Sasines (qv). *See* **registration for publication**.

sciens et prudens — in full knowledge; intentionally.

scienter — knowingly; the knowledge by the owner of an animal of its vicious nature, which formerly rendered him absolutely liable for damage caused by the animal. See now the Animals (Scotland) Act 1987.

scintilla juris — spark of law. Where there is no authority at all for a particular legal argument there is said to be no *scintilla juris* for it.

scire et scire debere aequiparantur in jure — to know a thing and to be bound to know it are the same thing in law. Ignorance of the law does not excuse any violation of it because everyone is bound and presumed to know the law of his own country.

Scots money. *See* **pound Scots**.

Scottish Land Court — a court set up under the Small Landholders (Scotland) Act 1911 with wide jurisdiction under Acts relating to agricultural holdings, smallholdings and crofts. The court comprises a legally qualified chairman with the status of a judge of the Court of Session and six other members experienced in agriculture, one of whom must speak Gaelic.

Scottish Law Commission — a body set up in 1965, comprising a chairman and not more than four other commissioners appointed by the Lord Advocate, to promote the reform of the law of Scotland by keeping the law under review and recommending codification, the elimination of anomalies, the repeal of unnecessary and obsolete enactments and generally the simplification and modernisation of the law. The Law Commission performs similar functions in respect of English law.

Scottish Office — all the departments of government under the control of the Secretary of State for Scotland.

Scottish Solicitors' Discipline Tribunal — a statutory tribunal established to investigate complaints of unprofessional conduct on the part of solicitors, inadequate professional services, breaches of the professional practice rules and the conviction of solicitors for serious crime, and to impose appropriate penalties or punishment.

scripto vel juramento — by writ or oath. In certain circumstances a party may be limited in attempting to prove his case to the production of his opponent's writings or, alternatively, referring to his oath. *See* **oath on reference**.

se defendendo — in defending himself; in self-defence (qv).

seal — a device fixed to or impressed on documents to symbolise authenticity. It is used primarily by corporate bodies and notaries public.

search for encumbrances —
  (1) an inspection of all relevant property and personal registers to trace the recording of the sequence of title deeds to heritable property and to ascertain the presence or otherwise of encumbrances (qv) affecting the property or restrictions on its disposition;
  (2) a document recording the results of such an inspection.

search warrant — a warrant to search for stolen goods or for other material or documents which might form evidence in criminal proceedings. It is granted by a sheriff or magistrate on the sworn evidence of the applicant.

secondary creditor — a creditor whose security ranks below those of another creditor. Cf **catholic creditor**.

Secretary of State for Scotland — the principal government minister concerned with Scottish affairs. He is responsible for the Scottish Office, is keeper of the Great Seal of Scotland, and has extensive powers and duties which range over the whole spectrum of government activities (eg education; environment; health; transport) for each of which, in England, there is a separate minister.

secundum ... — according to ...

secundum allegata et probata — according to what has been alleged and proved. The decision in every litigation must proceed upon the allegations of the parties and the evidence brought in support of them, and not upon the private knowledge of the judge. Cf *judicis est judicare secundum allegata et probata*.

secundum materiam subjectam — according to the subject matter.

secured creditor — a creditor holding a security for a debt, eg a standard security (qv) over heritable property.

security —
(1) something which tends to assure or to secure that an obligation will be performed, being either a personal security (eg a guarantee or cautionary obligation (qv) by a third party) or a real security where rights are granted over the debtor's property by pledge or heritable security;
(2) an investment, eg stocks and shares.

sed quaere — but inquire; an expression indicating doubt of the soundness of a judgment or proposition and suggesting further consideration.

sederunt — they sat; an attendance list, usually incorporated in the minutes of a meeting.

sederunt book — a record of the proceedings in a sequestration, maintained by the permanent trustee, and on his discharge lodged with the Accountant in Bankruptcy.

self-defence — a special defence to a criminal charge of homicidal assault. A person is entitled to use reasonable force to ward off an attack made upon him if there is no other way of escaping from the threatened violence.

semble — it seems: a word used to introduce a legal principle or proposition which is not quite clear but which appears to be implied in a particular judgment.

semper in dubiis benigniora praeferenda — in matters of doubt the more liberal view is always to be preferred: a rule of construction that, where the words used in a deed are doubtful or ambiguous, the most liberal interpretation is to be given to them so as to carry out what, from the deed itself, appears to have been the granter's intention. More generally, preference is to be given, in cases of doubt, to the most liberal or charitable view which the words, acts or circumstances in question will admit. Thus an accused person is always entitled to the benefit of a reasonable doubt of his guilt.

semper praesumitur pro negante — the presumption is always in favour of the person who denies. Thus the onus is always on the person who affirms. It is not always necessary (or, indeed, possible) to prove the negative.

Senator of the College of Justice — a judge of the Court of Session.

senior — of counsel, a Queen's Counsel (qv), as distinct from an advocate or junior counsel.

sentence —
(1) to impose a penalty on a person convicted of a crime or offence;
(2) the penalty thus imposed.

sententia interlocutoria revocari potest, definitiva non potest — an interlocutory judgment may be recalled, but a definitive judgment may not. Thus a judge may always recall or review a procedural decision issued by him in the course of a litigation, but he may not recall or review a definitive decision on any question of substance in the litigation submitted to him. In respect of such a definitive decision he is *functus officio* (qv).

separatim — separately; quite apart from anything argued or pleaded.

separation — the judicial separation, short of divorce, or spouses *a mensa et thoro* (qv).

sequestration —
(1) the process of rendering an individual bankrupt by attaching, ingathering and setting aside his assets, heritable and moveable, and vesting them in a trustee for the benefit of the bankrupt's creditors;
(2) generally, the judicial seizure of assets to enforce a claim or to satisfy a court order.

sequestration for rent — the seizure under the order of the sheriff court of a tenant's moveable property within his house for sale to satisfy his landlord's claim for arrears of rent. Such sequestration is the diligence to enforce the landlord's right of hypothec (qv).

seriatim — one by one; one after another.

series rerum judicatarum — a succession of decisions deciding some particular proposition or principle.

service —
- (1) the timeous delivery of a judicial writ or other formal document to another person in the prescribed manner as required by law;
- (2) the duty owed by an employee to his employer under a contract of service (*locatio operarum*) to do work in the manner directed by the employer, in contrast to a contract for services (*locatio operis faciendi*), where the employer has only limited control over the manner in which the services are performed and relies on the skill and expertise of the person hired;
- (3) an obsolete judicial process by which an heir's title to a deceased person's estate was established, being either general service, which determined the heir's general title without application to any particular property, or special service, which established his general title and his specific right to enter and be infeft in particular heritage;
- (4) the obsolete duty of a vassal to a feudal superior to perform certain personal services for him.

service mark — a mark (akin to a trade mark) used in relation to services, indicating that a particular person is connected in the course of business with the provision of those services.

servient tenement — land subject to a servitude in favour of the proprietor of other land, called the 'dominant tenement'.

servitude — an obligation attached to land, either restricting the owner's use of it (a 'negative servitude', eg limiting the height of buildings), or obliging the owner to allow others to exercise certain rights over it (a 'positive servitude'). Positive servitudes may be rural (eg a right of way over fields, or pasturage) or urban (eg support, eavesdrop or stillicide). *See also* **dominant tenement; servient tenement**.

sessions — the periods in a year, separated by vacations, during which the Court of Session and the sheriff courts sit to conduct civil business. The precise dates are fixed annually.

set-off. *See* **compensation**.

sett —
- (1) the constitution of a burgh (obsolete);
- (2) an action by a part owner of a ship seeking an order that the other part owners acquire his share or sell their shares to him, or that the ship be sold by public roup and the proceeds divided among the part owners.

settlement —
- (1) the termination of an action or legal dispute on agreed terms;
- (2) the completion of a transaction relating to heritable property;
- (3) a deed setting up a trust, *inter vivos* or *mortis causa*, to dispose of property subject to conditions and limitations;
- (4) the arrangement constituted by such a deed.

sheriff — originally the shire reeve; the holder of an ancient office who was the king's man in the shire or county. The office was hereditary until 1746, and comprised extensive military, financial, administrative and judicial functions. The sheriff is now the judge of a sheriff court with almost unlimited civil jurisdiction. Appeal from his judgment lies to the sheriff principal and the Inner House of the Court of Session. From his extensive criminal jurisdiction appeal lies to the High Court of Justiciary. Qualified persons may be appointed as temporary sheriffs. Honorary sheriffs, appointed by the sheriff principal, need not be legally qualified. They may relieve sheriffs of such duties as may be allocated to them.

sheriff clerk — the principal clerk of court in a sheriff court. He may be assisted by deputes and supported by ancillary staff.

sheriff court — the principal inferior court in Scotland, presided over by the sheriff (qv).

sheriff court district — the area which comprises the territorial jurisdiction of a sheriff court. *See also* **sheriffdom**.

sheriff officer — an officer of a sheriff court who is responsible for serving process and executing diligence. He is generally also a messenger-at-arms (qv).

sheriff principal — a judge, formerly known as a sheriff (qv), appointed to secure the speedy and efficient disposal of business in the sheriff courts throughout his sheriffdom. He hears appeals from sheriffs in civil cases, and appeal from him lies to the Inner House of the Court of Session.

sheriff substitute — the title, from 1746 to 1971, of the sheriff (qv).

sheriffdom — the area within which a sheriff principal exercises his jurisdiction. There are six such areas, each being divided into sheriff court districts.

shewer — one of two persons appointed by the Court of Session to accompany selected jurors in a civil case on a view of a place or other subject.

short roll. *See* **rolls**.

shorthand writer — a person who makes a verbatim shorthand note of the evidence given at a proof or trial.

si institutus sine liberis decesserit — if the beneficiary dies childless. *See* ***conditio si institutus sine liberis decesserit***.

si petitur tantum (or si petatur tantum) — if asked only; a payment which must be made only if the person entitled to it demands it, eg a nominal feuduty, such as one penny Scots or a peppercorn rent.

si sit incompos mentis, fatuus et naturaliter idiota — if of unsound mind, fatuous and naturally an idiot: the question which a jury formerly had to answer when considering the obsolete brieve of idiotry.

si (testator) sine liberis decesserit — if (the testator) has died without issue. *See* ***conditio si testator sine liberis decesserit***.

sic utere tuo ut alienum non laedas — use your own property so that you do not interfere with the natural rights of a neighbour.

Signet — the Queen's seal. *See* **Keeper of the Signet**.

Silk — a Queen's Counsel (qv), so called because he wears a silk gown.

simplex commendatio non obligat — a mere recommendation does not bind. Thus a buyer is not bound by a contract where he relied on inaccurate representations by the seller as to the quality of goods sold unseen.

simul et semel — at one and the same time.

sine — without.

sine animo remanendi — without the intention of remaining: used of a person who has left the country but who intends to return.

sine animo revertendi — without the intention of returning: used of a person who has left the country for good.

sine die — indefinitely; without a day being fixed eg for the resumption of adjourned proceedings.

sine qua non — without which nothing can effectually be done; an essential condition or factor;

sine quo non **trustee** — a trustee whose concurrence is required for all acts in the administration of the trust.

single bill roll — *See* **rolls**.

singular successor — a person who acquires the right to heritable property in some character other than by succession *mortis causa*. Thus a purchaser, a donee or a creditor acquiring heritage are all singular successors of the previous proprietor. Cf **universal successor**.

singuli in solidum — each is liable for the whole. *See* **conjunct and several obligation**.

sist —
(1) to stay or suspend court proceedings by order of the court;
(2) a stay or suspension of court proceedings;
(3) a court order staying or suspending legal proceedings;
(4) to interpose a person or to intervene in court proceedings as a litigant, eg as a third party with an interest intervening in a cause, as the executor of a deceased party or as the trustee or liquidator of an insolvent party.

skat — a tribute under udal tenure payable by udallers in Orkney or Shetland to the earl or to the Crown in right of the bishop (from the Norse *skattr* — tax; tribute). Future imposition of skat was prohibited in 1974.

sleep — the state into which a civil action fell when a year and a day had passed since the last step was taken in the procedure. In order to become operative again a minute of wakening was required.

small claims court — a court conducted by the sheriff for resolving small claims and petty disputes rapidly and inexpensively. It is about to be introduced in Scotland with particularly informal procedure.

small debt court — a court conducted before the sheriff or justices of the peace for the summary and inexpensive determination of petty claims. The sheriff's jurisdiction was latterly extended to £50 but was abolished in 1976 with the introduction of the summary cause (qv).

small tenancy — a tenancy of an agricultural holding controlled by the Crofters Acts as applied by the Small Landholders (Scotland) Acts.

societas — the contract of society or partnership.

socii — partners; associates.

socius criminis — an associate or accomplice in crime; *particeps criminis*.

solatium — compensation; damages given for injury to feelings or reputation, pain and suffering and loss of expectation of life. Awards of *solatium* to members of the immediate family of a deceased person were replaced by a loss of society award under the Damages (Scotland) Act 1976.

solemn procedure — the procedure under which a person charged with serious crime on indictment is tried before a sheriff or judge of the High Court of Justiciary with a jury of fifteen, whose decision to convict may be reached by at least eight votes.

solicitor — a member of the legal profession other than a member of the Faculty of Advocates, sometimes known as a law agent, a writer, a procurator or (in Aberdeen) an advocate. All practising solicitors in Scotland require to be members of the Law Society of Scotland.

Solicitor General for Scotland — a law officer of the Crown who assists the Lord Advocate and is a member of the government.

Solicitors in the Supreme Courts of Scotland (SSC) — a society of solicitors practising in the Court of Session, formed in 1784 and incorporated by royal charter in 1797.

solo animo — by the mere act of the mind; by mere intention or design. The law takes no cognisance of intent until it leads to some overt act. Thus an intention to steal is not criminal until it becomes at least an attempt.

solum — soil or ground, especially that on which a building stands.

solus cum sola in loco suspecto — a man alone with a woman in a suspicious place or circumstances. The circumstances may point to adultery.

sorner — one who begs importunately with threats; a scrounger; the subject of early poor law legislation.

souming and rouming; sowming and rowming — an action relating to the servitude of pasturage in which the extent of the pasturage and the proportion to be enjoyed by each commoner is determined.

special case —
  (1) proceedings to obtain, by consent, the opinion of the Inner House of the Court of Session on a point of law when the parties agree as to the facts;
  (2) a form of statutory appeal by which the opinion of the Court of Session may be obtained on a point of law referred to it by an inferior court, eg the Scottish Land Court or the sheriff principal sitting as an election court.

special defence — a defence (eg alibi, insanity, incrimination or self-defence) notice of which must be given to the prosecutor before the beginning of a criminal trial.

special destination — a provision in a will or the title to heritable property indicating or directing some departure from the legally implied line of succession *mortis causa*.

special service. *See* **service** (3).

special verdict — the verdict of a jury in a civil trial making findings of fact to enable the court to apply the appropriate law, as distinct from a verdict determining the specific issues raised.

species facti — the particular nature of the thing done; the precise circumstances attending any alleged crime or civil wrong.

specific implement; specific performance — the performance of a contractual or common law obligation, other than by the payment of money. It is enforced by decree *ad factum praestandum* (qv), but damages may be awarded instead.

specificatio — acquisition of property by changing the formation of materials belonging to another into a new species, eg by making flour out of corn or wine out of grapes.

specification — in written pleadings, the full and proper description of the facts and circumstances and the legal propositions upon which a party founds. A lack of specification may be pled in an attack upon the relevancy of pleadings and may lead to the dismissal of an action or defence.

spei emptio — the purchase of a hope or chance, eg of the right of succession or the produce of the cast of a net.

spes obligationis — the hope or expectation of a future obligation.

spes successionis — the hope or expectation of future succession. It has a market value and may be used for security.

spoliatus ante omnia restituendus — a person despoiled is to be restored to his possession first. Thus a person violently deprived of goods of which he is in lawful possession may recover them on proving that lawful possession, even against the true owner, before questions of right are considered.

spondet peritiam artis et imperitia culpae enumeratur — a person is responsible for exercising skill in his profession, and want of such skill will be regarded as a fault. Thus an employer is entitled to assume that a person will display the skill which he professes, up to a reasonable standard.

sponsiones ludicrae — obligations in jest; an agreement unenforceable because the parties did not seriously intend to be bound in law, eg a betting or gaming contract.

spuilzie (pronounced 'spool(y)i') —
(1) the carrying off of, or intermeddling with, the moveable property of another without his consent;
(2) a civil action for the restoration of spuilzied property and damages for consequential loss.

stabit praesumptio donec probetur in contrarium — the presumption will stand until the contrary is proved: a general rule providing that those who have the benefit of a presumption will retain it until it is overcome by proof to the contrary.

Stair Society — a learned society founded in 1934 to encourage the study and knowledge of the history of the law of Scotland and to publish books on aspects of the subject.

stamp duty — a tax on a legal document, the payment of which, evidenced by impressing or affixing an official stamp, is generally essential to the enforceability of the obligations constituted by the document.

standard charge. *See* **stipend**.

standard conditions — statutory conditions which, subject to variations agreed by the parties, regulate a standard security (qv).

standard security — the only form in which an interest in land for the purpose of securing a debt by way of a heritable security may now be created. It is not effective until recorded in the General Register of Sasines or registered in the Land Register of Scotland.

stare decisis — to stand upon decisions; to abide by precedents.

stated case — an appeal procedure by which the decision of an inferior court or tribunal may be referred to the Court of Session or the High Court of Justiciary so that that court may pronounce on questions of law arising. In the procedure the lower court 'states a case for the opinion of' the appeal court.

status — the legal standing or position of a person, eg as a minor, single person, widow etc, upon which may depend his or her legal capacity.

status quo — the existing or present situation or state of affairs.

status quo ante — the situation or state of affairs which existed before a particular date or event.

statute — an Act of Parliament, public or private, made by the Sovereign by and with the advice and consent of Parliament and by its authority.

statutory instruments (SI) — the form in which orders, rules, regulations or other subordinate legislation are made. Statutory instruments are prescribed or enacted under the royal prerogative or statutory authority by the Queen in Council or a minister of the Crown.

statutory rules and orders (SR & O) — the form in which subordinate legislation was made until the end of 1947. Thereafter they took the form of statutory instruments (qv).

steelbow — a practice by which the landlord of a farm stocked the farm on an undertaking by his tenant to restore their equivalents at the end of the lease.

stellionate — any fraudulent or deceitful act (obsolete).

stent — a tax or duty.

stillicide. *See* **eavesdrop**.

stipend — the remuneration of a parish minister which was formerly met out of a standard charge upon local heritable property, and formerly based on teinds (qv). It must now be redeemed upon sale.

stipendiary magistrate — a salaried legally qualified magistrate appointed by a local authority to be a judge in a district court.

stoppage in transit — the statutory right of an unpaid seller of goods who has parted with possession of the goods to stop them in transit if the buyer becomes insolvent, and to resume possession of them and retain them pending payment.

stouthrief — robbery (qv) aggravated by housebreaking or mob violence.

strict liability — absolute liability regardless of fault. The principle of strict liability for loss or damage arises in certain circumstances in the civil law. It also arises under statute in the criminal law in certain circumstances where something is done or allowed to happen without any intention or negligence or, sometimes, even knowledge.

stricti juris — according to strict right or law.

style —
  (1) the name or title of a person;
  (2) an approved form of a document, used as a model for drawing up similar documents.

sua sponte — voluntarily; of one's own free will.

sub judice — in the hands of the law. A matter or dispute which is *sub judice* has been brought before a court in a litigation for decision, but the decision has not yet been given.

sub modo — under condition or restriction. Thus property may be conveyed to a trustee under condition that it be applied for certain specified purposes.

subfeuar — a person who holds heritable property by subinfeudation (qv).

subinfeudation — the grant of a sub-feu by a feudal proprietor out of his heritable estate. Prohibitions against subinfeudation are void.

subjects — property, generally heritable, although the expression can sometimes and in certain contexts comprehend moveables.

submission — a contract entered into between two or more parties who have debatable rights or claims against one another, by which they refer their differences to the final determination of an arbiter and oblige themselves to acquiesce in his decision.

subordinate legislation — Orders in Council, orders, rules, regulations, schemes, warrants, byelaws and other instruments made, or to be made, under the authority of an Act of Parliament.

subornation of perjury — the crime of inducing a witness to commit perjury (qv).

subrogation — the principle under which a person who has discharged another's liabilities is entitled to any related claims or rights of relief vested in that other.

subsequente copula — with subsequent carnal intercourse. Prior to 1940 intercourse allowed on the faith of a promise of marriage constituted a valid irregular marriage.

substitute — a person named as beneficiary in case the institute (qv) fails.

succession — the passing of property from one person to another, especially on the death of the owner, governed by deed or will or, on an intestacy, by statutory rules. Succession may be universal, under which the whole of the property, with its rights and liabilities, passes together (eg to the executor of a deceased person or a trustee on bankruptcy), or singular, where particular items of property pass to a specific person such as a purchaser or donee.

sue — to raise a civil action against a person.

sui juris — of full legal capacity, describing a person not under a legal disability such as minority, pupillarity or insanity.

summar roll. *See* **rolls**.

summary application — an application to a sheriff which may be disposed of either forthwith or in accordance with a summary and swift procedure prescribed by the sheriff.

summary cause — a civil action in the sheriff court seeking payment or the delivery of goods to the value of £1,000. It is commenced by summons under and follows the simplified procedure set out in the Summary Cause Rules.

summary decree — a decree granted by the Court of Session on the application of the pursuer in an action where the defences lodged disclose no defence to the action.

summary diligence — diligence proceedings to enforce the payment of a debt without the necessity of an action to constitute the debt. It is employed to enforce payment of bills of exchange, promissory notes, rates etc.

summary petition. *See* **summary trial**.

summary proceedings — criminal proceedings taken before a sheriff, magistrate or justice sitting alone, ie without a jury.

summary removing — a procedure by which, where heritable property is let for a shorter period than a year, the sheriff may on summary application pronounce a decree for removing.

summary sequestration — an adaptation of the normal sequestration procedure formerly used where a debtor's assets did not exceed £300. It has now been replaced by a modified procedure under Schedule 2 of the Bankruptcy (Scotland) Act 1985 for small estates or for sequestrations where the creditors do not elect a permanent trustee.

summary suspension — the sisting of diligence by the sheriff on the summary application of a party.

summary taxation — the taxation (qv) of a solicitor's account by the Auditor of Court on a remit by the Court of Session granted on the summary application of the client or the solicitor during the dependence of the process in court or following decree.

summary trial —
   (1) the trial of a dispute or question in the Outer House of the Court of Session by consent of the parties on application initiated by summary petition, held either in court or in chambers by an agreed simplified procedure;
   (2) the trial of an accused person under summary proceedings (qv).

summary trial rolls. *See* **rolls**.

summary warrant — a warrant issued by the sheriff to a local authority authorising diligence for the recovery of arrears of rates or community charges.

summons — a document requiring a person to appear in court to answer a claim made against him.

summum jus, summa injuria — extreme right is extreme injury. Thus to give one person everything he is entitled to may inflict great harm on another. This principle is a restraint in equity on the strict enforcement of a legal right or obligation.

suo nomine — in one's own name.

suo periculo — at one's own risk. *See* ***periculo petentis***.

superior — in feudal tenure the person holding heritable property immediately from the Crown (the paramount superior) who grants land to a vassal in return for the payment of feuduty. The vassal then holds the *dominium utile* (qv) and the superior retains the *dominium directum* (qv). The vassal may in turn, as mediate superior, grant land to a sub-vassal, and so on, without limit. Feuduties may no longer be created and must be redeemed on sale.

supersede —
  (1) to postpone for a period, as of an extract for a decree;
  (2) to replace.

support —
  (1) the right of the owner of land to such support from beside or below it as is necessary to uphold it in its natural state;
  (2) a servitude entitling the proprietor of the dominant tenement to rest the weight of his building on the wall of the servient tenement.

supra — above.

supra citatum — above cited (generally abbreviated '*sup cit*'), a phrase used to refer to a matter earlier or already cited.

surrogatum — a surrogate or substitute.

surrogatum capit naturam rei surrogati — a thing substituted partakes of the nature or character of that for which it was substituted.

survivorship clause — a clause in a will or conveyance by which a testator or granter provides that should one of several beneficiaries or grantees die before he takes, his interest is to pass to the survivor or those who survive.

suspension — the means by which injury of rights, occasioned or threatened by court decrees, sentences or orders and diligence, is prevented, namely:
  (1) a procedure in the Court of Session or sheriff court to stay the execution of diligence or threatened diligence (*see also* **suspension and interdict**);
  (2) a procedure in the Court of Session to recall a decree granted *in absentia*;
  (3) a procedure in the Court of Session to recall the decree of an inferior court;
  (4) a procedure by which an illegal warrant or summary conviction in criminal proceedings in the sheriff court or the district court may be set aside by the High Court of Justiciary.

suspension and interdict —
  (1) a procedure in the Court of Session to stay the execution of diligence where injury has taken place, eg where there has been a poinding (if a sale of the poinded goods has been obtained, the remedy is suspension and suspension and interdict);
  (2) a procedure in the Court of Session to prevent injury to a right by a deliberate act which is threatened or is being performed.

suspension and liberation — a procedure in the Court of Session for release from imprisonment for civil debt.

suspensive condition — a condition which prevents an obligation arising unless and until a specific future event, certain or uncertain, occurs. Cf **resolutive condition**.

suum cuique tribuere — to give to everyone that which is his own: one of the three principles laid down by Justinian (Institutes I, 1, 3) as those upon which all rules of law are based. '*Suum cuique*' is the motto of the Faculty of Advocates.

t

tabling — the stage in an ordinary action in the sheriff court at which, notice of intention to defend having been given, the pursuer or his solicitor attends court on the day appointed and tables, ie presents or lodges with the sheriff clerk, the initial writ, interlocutor sheets and other documents which constitute the process (qv). If the pursuer fails to do so the defender may crave protestation and thus compel the pursuer either to proceed with or abandon the action.

tacit relocation — implied consent to the renewal of a lease if notice to terminate the lease is not given timeously. The renewal is for one year in the case of a lease for a year or more or, in the case of a lease for a shorter term, for that term. The principle applies also to certain contracts of service and (save that the renewal is indefinite) to partnerships.

taciturnity — silence of the creditor which raises a presumption that, in the relative situations of himself and the debtor, and in all the circumstances, the creditor would not have been so long silent if the debt had not been paid or other obligation implemented. *See also* **mora taciturnity and acquiescence**.

tack —
   (1) a lease or tenancy, especially of a farm or a mill (obsolescent);
   (2) the land held on a tack;
   (3) a payment levied by a feudal superior (obsolete).

tack duty or takkar duty — the rent paid by a tacksman.

tacksman — the lessee under a tack.

tailzie *or* **tailyie** (pronounced 'tile(y)i'). *See* **entail**.

takkar — the person who granted a tack.

tanquam quilibet — like any other person. The Sovereign or an official may have certain prerogatives, but in ordinary matters, such as buying and selling property, they act *tanquam quilibet*.

tantum et tale — so much and of such a kind. Subjects so described when sold are accepted by the buyer with all their advantages and faults, just as they are.

tantum praescriptum quantum possessum — there is only one prescription in so far as there has been possession. Thus continuous possession for the appropriate period is an essential prerequisite for the operation of prescription.

taxation — the scrutiny of a solicitor's account for legal expenses or charges in litigation by the Auditor of Court.

teind (pronounced 'teend') — tithe; one-tenth of the annual produce of land, originally used towards the support of the clergy, and after the Reformation towards the minister's stipend. Since 1925 teinds have been standardised at a fixed standard charge.

Teind Clerk — the officer of the Court of Session, acting under the direction of the Principal Clerk of Session, in charge of the Teind Office, which is responsible for all processes dealt with by the Teind Court and the Lord Ordinary on Teinds. *See* **Commissioner of Teinds**.

Teind Court. *See* **Commissioner of Teinds**.

temere litigare — to litigate rashly or without reasonable ground.

tempus continuum — time running on without interruption during which a legal right may be exercised or not.

tempus mortis inspiciendum — the time of death is to be regarded. Thus in considering the effect of a will, it is the date of the testator's death which is important, not the date of the will. Accordingly a legacy bequeathed to a person who predeceased the testator lapses and becomes ineffectual.

tenancy — a right of occupation under a lease (qv).

tenant — a person who occupies in terms of a lease (qv) heritable property belonging to a landlord (qv) to whom the tenant pays periodic rent. The occupation in terms of the tenancy is for a fixed (usually renewable) period and the contract is normally subject to a number of additional terms and conditions.

tender —
   (1) to offer money in payment of a debt or liability, especially (by a defender) to offer money, with expenses, in settlement of an action for the payment of damages (upon refusal of which a pursuer who is subsequently awarded only the amount tendered or less will be liable for the defender's expenses from the date of the tender);
   (2) money so offered.
See also **legal tender**.

tenement —
  (1) heritable property having the benefit of or burdened by a servitude (*see* **dominant tenement** and **servient tenement**);
  (2) a building containing several dwellinghouses under the same roof, sometimes with common staircases and means of access, and thus combining separate ownership with common interest, regulated by special rules known as 'the law of the tenement'.

tenendas — the clause in a feu charter which sets forth the nature of the tenure (qv) by which the land is to be held.

tenor. *See* **proving the tenor**.

tenure — the relationship between the superior and the vassal in the feudal system of holding heritable property. There were a number of different forms of tenure, such as ward (involving military service), burgage (burgh lands), blench (with nominal returns) and, most popularly, feu ferme (payment in money and goods).

terce — liferent of one-third of the heritage of a deceased husband conferred on a widow who has not accepted provision under his will (obsolete since 1964).

term —
  (1) a condition or stipulation in an agreement;
  (2) a fixed period, especially the period during which an agreement is to subsist;
  (3) a fixed date, especially the date on which a person must pay interest or rent, the legal terms for payment being Whitsunday (qv) and Martinmas (qv).

term of entry — the date on which a tenant or the purchaser of heritage enters into possession under a lease or under missives (qv).

terminus a quo — the point from which, used especially in expressing when a period of time begins.

terminus ad quem — the point at which; used especially in expressing when a period of time ends.

termly — (adj or adv) at each term.

tertium quid — a third thing, having a character and qualities distinct from those of either of its two components. Thus where liquids are confused or solids are commixed the subject produced, being different from the other two, is a *tertium quid*.

tertius — a third party (qv).

testament — a will.

testamentary writing — a will or codicil.

testament-dative — the former name for the confirmation of an executor dative (qv).

testament-testamentar — the former name for the confirmation of an executor nominate (qv).

testate —
  (1) (adj) having died leaving a valid will for the disposal, in whole or in part, of the estate of the deceased;
  (2) a person who dies having left such a document.

testator — a person who dies leaving a valid will for the disposal of his estate.

testibus non testimoniis credendum est — credence should be given to the witness, not to his evidence. The character and credibility of a witness is more important than the probability or otherwise of what he says. Thus an improbable fact spoken to by an unimpeachable witness is more likely to be accepted than a probable fact spoken to by a doubtful or incredible witness.

testimonia ponderanda sunt, non numeranda — the evidence of witnesses is to be weighed, not counted. Thus the character and quality of the evidence given is more important than the number of witnesses who give it.

testimony — oral evidence given in court.

testing clause — the attestation clause at the end of a deed identifying any erasures or alterations, specifying the date and place of execution and naming and designating the witnesses.

theft — the crime of dishonestly taking and keeping the property of another person without his consent.

Thellusson Act — The Accumulations Act 1800 (now replaced by the Trusts (Scotland) Act 1961, s 5), which, as amended, prohibits or restricts accumulations of income by trustees.

third party —
(1) a *tertius*; a person who, not being a party to a transaction between others (and who would consequently more correctly be called a 'third person'), is nevertheless in some way connected with or affected by that transaction, and who in appropriate circumstances may have a *jus quaesitum tertio* (qv) conferred on him by a contract between those other people;
(2) a person who, not originally being a party to a civil action in the Court of Session or the sheriff court, is added as a party by leave of the court, commonly on the application of a defender who claims that he has a right of contribution, relief or indemnity against the third party or that the third party should be made a party along with the defender as being solely liable or jointly and severally liable with him.

third party notice — a notice served on a third party setting out the defender's claim against him and requiring him to lodge answers within a specified period.

thirlage — a burden akin to a servitude by which land was formerly astricted or thirled to a particular mill, to which grain produced on the land had to be taken for grinding, for the payment of multures (qv).

thole — to suffer, endure or be subjected to.

thole an assize — to stand or suffer trial. Once an accused person has tholed his assize on a criminal charge he may not be tried again on the same charge.

tigni immittendi — an urban servitude permitting the dominant proprietor to fix a beam or joist in the wall of the servient tenement.

time bar — the effect of lapse of time on a person's rights, preventing his taking steps to enforce those rights or extinguishing them entirely. *See also* **prescription.**

timeous — within the period allowed by law.

tinsel — the forfeiture of a right or its termination by default in performing some condition.

tinsel of superiority — the forfeiture of all or some of the rights of superiorities on declarator of the superior's failure to complete his defective title.

tinsel of the feu — the forfeiture of a vassal's rights for failure to pay feuduties. *See **ob non solutum canonem.***

tithe — the tenth part of the produce, direct or indirect, of land, extricable for the maintenance of the church and the clergy. Tithes continued to be exacted after the Reformation, and were latterly called 'teinds' (qv).

title —
(1) the right to the ownership of property;
(2) the deed or other instrument constituting evidence of that right;
(3) a personal designation denoting some office, honour or dignity;
(4) the name or heading of an Act of Parliament, deed, writ, book or document.

title deed — a deed or other instrument constituting evidence of the ownership of heritable property.

title to sue — a legal right to raise an action.

titular —
(1) a layman to whom the Crown transferred the title to church land after the Reformation;
(2) (adj) having a title, if only in name.

titulus transferendi dominii — the cause or intention of conveying property, as opposed to *modus transferendi,* which is the form of conveying property.

tocher *or* **toucher** — a marriage portion or dowry.

tocher band — a marriage settlement.

tota re perspecta — the whole matter being clearly in view; in all the circumstances.

toties quoties — as often as; for each time.

totting up — the accumulation of penalty points imposed and recorded in a driving licence after convictions for motoring offences. The accumulation of twelve penalty points involves automatic disqualification for holding a driving licence.

trade description — a direct or indirect indication of the quantity, quality, composition or fitness for their purpose of goods supplied or offered in the course of a trade or business. The application or use of a false trade description is an offence.

trade mark — a mark on goods indicating a connection in the course of trade between goods and the person entitled to use the mark. If registered, the mark is a certification trade mark.

traditio — handing over; delivery.

traditionibus (et usucapionibus), non nudis pactis, transferuntur rerum dominia — rights of property are transferred by delivery (and by prescription), and not by mere agreement. See, however, the Sale of Goods Act 1979.

transfer —
(1) to convey or voluntarily hand over property or rights in property from one person to another (cf **transmission**);
(2) to remove an action from one court to another, or from one roll to another within the same court;
(3) to effect a transference (qv);
(4) a document effecting a transfer, eg of shares in a company.

transference — the process in the Court of Session whereby an action by or against a person is reconstituted upon his death, bankruptcy, insanity or otherwise so that it becomes an action by or against another, eg his executor, trustee or curator.

transmission —
(1) the transfer of legal rights from one person to another, eg on bankruptcy or death;
(2) the transfer of proceedings from one court to another;
(3) the sending of documents from one place (eg a court) to another.

transumpts —
(1) an extract, duplicate or copy of a writ or a portion thereof made or recovered for production in a litigation (obsolete);
(2) an action to recover a deed in the hands of a third person so that a transumpt could be made of it (obsolete).

treason — a crime committed by compassing the death of the Sovereign or the Sovereign's consort or heir, by violating the Queen, the Sovereign's eldest daughter unmarried or the wife of the Sovereign's heir, by making war against the Sovereign within the realm, by adhering to the Sovereign's enemies or giving them aid or comfort, by disputing or hindering the succession to the Crown, by killing any judge of the Court of Session or the High Court of Justiciary whilst exercising his office, or by counterfeiting seals kept under the Act of Union of 1707.

treasure trove — coin, gold, silver, plate and bullion found in the ground, apparently abandoned, the owner being unknown. As a sub-category of ownerless things it may be claimed by the Crown, but as a matter of grace – and policy – the Crown may reward the finder.

trespass — a temporary intrusion upon the land of another without permission or legal justification. Damages are not recoverable for mere trespass in Scotland. The only remedy is interdict. Trespass has a much wider meaning in English law.

trial —
(1) the hearing of a criminal case in court;
(2) the hearing of a civil case in court before a judge and jury. Cf **proof** (1).

tribunal — a court, especially a person or body of persons appointed under statute to hear and determine particular questions. Thus entitlement to redundancy payments, compensation on the compulsory acquisition of land, social security benefits and the like are determined by tribunals. *See* eg **Lands Tribunal for Scotland.**

trust — a legal concept under which property is granted to or vested in a trustee or trustees by deed, will or operation of law in the confidence that they will so administer it that the beneficial interest will be applied to or enjoyed by nominated persons or purposes.

trust deed — a deed constituting a trust (qv).

trust deed for creditors — a deed by which an insolvent person conveys his estate to trustees for the benefit of his creditors. By statute the deed may be protected against the possibility of being suspended by sequestration proceedings.

trustee —
(1) a person administering a trust (qv);
(2) a person in whom the legal title to property is vested in trust for others, eg as an executor of the estate of a deceased person.

As to trustees in a sequestration, *see* **interim trustee** and **permanent trustee.**

truster — a person who creates a trust (qv) to control and manage property belonging to him.

turpis causa — an immoral or illegal purpose. Contracts for such a purpose are unenforceable.

tutius semper est errare ex parte misericordiae quam ex parte justitiae — it is safer to err on the side of mercy than of justice. Thus it is better that ten guilty men should go unpunished than that one innocent man should suffer unjustly.

tutius semper est errare in acquietando quam in puniendo — it is safer to err in acquitting than in punishing. *See* ***tutius semper est errare ex parte misericordiae quam ex parte justitiae.***

tutor *or* **tutrix** — the guardian of a pupil (qv).

tutor *ad litem* — a tutor appointed to safeguard a pupil's interests in legal proceedings.

tutor-at-law — a pupil's nearest male relative on his father's side, who becomes tutor in default of any appointment by the parents.

tutor dative — a tutor appointed by the Court of Session or the sheriff court.

tutor datur personae, curator rei — a tutor is appointed to take care of a pupil's person, a curator to preserve a minor's estate.

tutor nominate — a tutor named by the parents of a pupil.

tutory — the guardianship and legal representation of a pupil.

u

uberrimae fidei — with perfect frankness; in utmost good faith; the standard required in certain contracts, especially for insurance, although generally this is required more of the insured than of the insurer!

ubi id non agebatur — where that was not done.

ubi jus ibi remedium — where there is a right, there is a remedy, ie a right of action to protect the right.

ubi onus ibi emolumentum — where there is a burden, there is a profit or advantage. Thus rights and obligations go together.

udal tenure — a form of land tenure, formerly common in Northern Europe, and surviving in parts of Orkney and Shetland. Those islands were pledged in the 15th century in security of the unpaid dowry of Princess Margaret of Norway and Denmark, wife of James III. Landowners (udallers) paid skat (tax) to the Crown under udal law (Code of Magnus the Lawmender). In 1974 future imposition of skat was prohibited. Most land in Orkney and Shetland is now held on feudal tenure.

ultimo loco — in the last place.

ultimus haeres — the last heir. On an intestacy the Crown takes as *ultimus haeres* if there are no other heirs, but may confer the residue on relatives or others by way of gift.

ultra fines compromissi — beyond the limits of the submission or reference; grounds for partial or complete reduction of an arbiter's decision.

ultra petita — beyond that which was sought. A judge cannot award more than is asked for or sued for in a litigation.

ultra vires — beyond the powers. Thus acts or deeds of those to whom powers are granted may be reduced if they exceed the substance of the delegated powers or if requisite procedures have not been observed. The term is used especially in the context of delegated legislation and the activities of central and local government, trustees and companies.

ultra vires compromissi — beyond the force or import of the submission. *See* **ultra fines compromissi.**

ultroneous — spontaneous; voluntary; as of a witness, without having been cited.

umpire. *See* **oversman.**

umquhile (pronounced 'umwhile') —
(1) (of a person) former; late; deceased;
(2) formerly.

undefended cause or action — an action in court in which the defender has failed to appear to contest it.

unfair contract terms — extreme contractual terms excluding or restricting liability for breach of contract. They were rendered void or voidable by the Unfair Contract Terms Act 1977.

unfair dimissal — a statutory ground for complaint by an employee to an industrial tribunal which, if established, may involve the employer in paying compensation or reinstating or re-engaging the employee.

unfair preference — an agreement voluntarily entered into by a debtor who is knowingly insolvent which has the effect of creating a preference in favour of a creditor to the prejudice of the general body of creditors. Such a preference was formerly misleadingly known as a 'fraudulent preference'.

unfit to plead — the state of a person accused of crime who by reason of his mental condition is not capable of understanding his trial. If the accused is unfit to plead his trial cannot take place. If the Crown proposed nevertheless to proceed with the case a preliminary plea of insanity in bar of trial would be made.

unico contextu — in one connection; by one and the same act; as part of a single continuous process. Thus multiple parties to a deed need not execute it *unico contextu,* at the same time and place, but a granter and his witness must so subscribe it.

unilateral — involving only one person. Thus a will or gift is a unilateral transaction, whereas a contract between two parties is bilateral.

unincorporated association — a voluntary association comprising a body or society of persons who have come together for the purpose of business or trade, as a partnership or firm, or for some sporting, charitable, religious, scientific or leisure purpose.

United Kingdom — Great Britain (ie Scotland, England and Wales) and Northern Ireland.

universal successor — a person (eg an heir) who succeeds to the entire estate, rights and liabilities of a deceased person. Cf **singular successor.**

universitas — the whole; the entire property of an individual; an undivided collection.

unjust enrichment — the priniciple that a person who receives an unmerited and unjustifiable benefit to another person's loss should recompense that other person. It is the principle behind quasi-contractual obligations.

unum quid — one thing. The phrase is applicable where several things are for some purpose or reason taken and considered and treated together as one.

unumquodque eodem modo dissolvitur quo colligatur — an obligation is discharged in the same manner as that in which it was constituted. Thus verbal agreements may be discharged verbally, but those constituted in writing may in general only be discharged in writing.

uplift — to collect or take possession of something, especially money.

upset price — the minimum price set for property put up for auction, below which bids will not be accepted (in England, the reserve price). The upset price is usually advertised before the auction.

urban — relating to a dwellinghouse or other building in a town or city, eg an urban lease, or an urban servitude as opposed to a rural servitude.

urban development area — an area of land in a town or city designated by the Secretary of State as one in need of regeneration by an urban development corporation, which may be empowered to exercise certain local authority functions eg over planning, building control, housing and public health.

usucapio or **usucapion** — the acquisition of property under the civil law by lengthened possession similar to positive prescription (qv).

usufruct — liferent (qv).

usus — use; usage; custom.

usus fit ex iteratis actibus — uses that arise from repeated acts. A right acquired by use cannot be acquired by a single act: the act must be repeated before a series of acts can be held to amount to a use.

ususfructus — liferent (qv).

ut intus — as within: a reference in one part of a book or document to a statement in another part of it.

ut res valeat potius quam pereat — in order that the thing may avail rather than perish: a rule to give a benign interpretation to documents so as to avoid defeating their purpose.

ut supra — as above.

ut voluntas testatoris sortiatur effectum — that effect may be given to the will of a testator. If the trustee dies or declines to act, the court will appoint a judicial factor (qv) to give effect to the will.

uterine — descended from the same mother but not the same father, eg half brother. Cf **consanguinean.**

uttering — the crime of tendering a forged document or banknote or a counterfeit coin with the necessary criminal intention, whether or not the result intended is achieved.

uxor sequitur domicilium viri — a wife follows her husband's domicile. The proposition is not necessarily true today.

V

vacant possession — the state of heritable property which is available for sale with legal possession and which has nothing and no person (such as a tenant) in occupation to prevent a purchaser enjoying actual possession.

vacation — a period between sessions (qv) of the court; a recess during which the court is not generally sitting.

vacation court — a court sitting during vacation.

vacation judge — a judge sitting during vacation. In the Court of Session the judges (other than the Lord President and the Lord Justice-Clerk) sit in rotation as vacation judge to hear urgent business.

valens agere — able to act; describes a person of full age and full legal capacity. The negative is *non valens agere*. Prescription did not run against a person so described.

valentia agendi — the power or capacity to act.

vassal — in feudal tenure the owner of the *dominium utile* (qv) of land, his right of ownership being conditional on his fulfilling certain obligations imposed by his superior (qv). He is often termed 'proprietor' in modern practice.

verba accipienda sunt secundum subjectam materiam — words are to be accepted according to the subject matter of which they deal; words are to be understood in context.

verba debent intelligi cum effectu ut res magis valeat quam pereat— words ought to be read or understood as of some effect, so that the matter (ie the deed, contract etc in which the words are used) may be of some avail rather than perish. Thus, if two interpretations are possible, the one to be preferred is that which makes sense.

verba jactantia — empty, vain words; words spoken in jest.

verba sollennia — solemn or formal words; words essential to validity. At one time the word 'dispone' in a disposition was of that character.

verbal injury — the actionable wrongs of injurious words. Though intent to insult (*animus injuriandi*) was regarded as essential irrespective of patrimonial loss, some decisions have used the expression to apply to causing loss by a false but not slanderous statement.

verbatim et literatim — word for word and letter for letter; an exact copy. The phrase is usually abbreviated '*verbatim*'.

verdict — the decision of a jury.

vergens ad inopiam — approaching to want; tending to insolvency. Formerly a creditor could resort to certain measures to protect his interests if the debtor was *vergens ad inopiam*.

veritas convicii — the truth of the accusation, a defence to an action of defamation.

verity — truth. In a sequestration an oath of verity that his claim was true was formerly required from a creditor.

versans in illicito — engaged in some unlawful occupation; performing an illegal act.

vest — to become the property of a person, and thus transmissible to heirs and assignees. In succession, vesting may depend on survival to an ascertainable date, eg three months after the testator's death. Cf mere *spes successionis*.

vexatious litigant — a person who brings proceedings primarily for the purpose of annoying or embarrassing the defender. The Court of Session may prohibit the institution of proceedings by a vexatious litigant unless the court's approval has first been obtained.

vi aut clam aut precario — by force, by clandestine stealth or by importunate entreaty. Possession of property obtained by any of these means is regarded as precarious possession.

vi et metu — by force and fear. Contracts so induced are probably void or voidable according to circumstances; marriages so induced are null.

vicarious liability — the liability of a person for the delictual act or omission of an employee, servant or agent. The vicarious liability is additional to the liability of the actual wrongdoer. *See* **qui facit per alium facit per se**.

vice versa — conversely.

vicennial prescription — prescription (qv) for twenty years.

vide infra — see below.

vide supra — see above.

videlicet — namely, usually abbreviated as 'viz'.

view — an inspection outwith the court by a judge or a jury of premises which are the subject matter of a litigation.

vigilantibus non dormientibus jura subveniunt — the law assists those who are watchful of their rights, not those who are careless of them. Thus prescription cancels rights which are not enforced over prescribed periods.

vindicatio — a real action. In Roman law, an action competent to an owner against anyone in actual possession. In Scots law it is sometimes used loosely in relation to claims to the ownership of corporeal moveables.

violent profits — penal damages exigible as a deterrent against a tenant unwarrantably ('violently') taking or retaining possession of heritable property. In urban property they are estimated at double the rent; elsewhere they are the greatest rent the landlord could have obtained, together with compensation for any damage.

vis et metus — force and fear. *See* **vi et metu**.

vis major — greater or superior power; *force majeure*.

visitation —
(1) a visit to a parish by the presbytery to exercise supervision, for judicial or administrative purposes or to express sympathy;
(2) the examination of records by a superior court.

visiting force — the naval, military or air force of one of certain designated countries whose members are by statute subject to the service courts of the sending country and not to the courts of the host country.

vitious intromitter — a person who, by taking possession, without authority, of the property of a deceased person, incurs unlimited liability for all the debts of the deceased.

vitium reale — a real defect. *See* **labes realis quae rei inhaeret.**

viva voce — orally.

viz. *See* ***videlicet.***

voces signatae — formal words; words with a special technical meaning.

void — null; having no legal effect whatsoever, eg a purported marriage by a person under age.

voidable — apparently valid, but vitiated in some way, so that a contract, deed or obligation may be annulled or set aside by the person entitled to avoid it. Until so avoided the subject remains valid.

volenti non fit injuria — no wrong is done to him who consents: the principle that a person who voluntarily (either expressly or impliedly) accepts the risk of an injury which he in fact sustains cannot then claim damages. This is a defence in an action of damages for personal injury or death.

voluntas est ambulatoria usque ad mortem — a will is ambulatory until death takes place. It may thus be altered or revoked at any time during the lifetime of the testator.

voluntas testatoris — the intention of the testator.

vouch — to confirm or answer for something.

voucher —
(1) a document or receipt confirming the payment of money;
(2) the document to be exchanged for goods or services, implying that payment has already been made.

vox emissa volat; litera scripta manet — the spoken word is transitory; writing remains. The spoken word may be forgotten, misunderstood and misrepresented, but a document speaks for itself and remains the same.

W

W S — Writer to the Signet. *See* **Writer.**

wadset — the obsolete conveyance of land to a creditor (the 'wadsetter') in security for or in satisfaction of a debt or other obligation with a reserved power to the debtor (the 'reverser') to recover the land on payment or performance.

waiver — an express or implied voluntary renunciation or forsaking of the assertion of a right. A superior may expressly renounce or modify conditions in a feu charter by a minute of waiver.

wakening. *See* **sleep.**

ward — a person of limited legal capacity, such as a pupil, minor or person of unsound mind, on whose behalf legal steps are taken by a tutor or curator.

ward holding — the obsolete feudal tenure of land in exchange for military service.

warn — to notify the other party of intention to terminate a lease or contract of service.

warrandice — an express or implied personal obligation (personal warrandice) of a granter (eg a seller or lessor), especially of heritable property, to indemnify the granter in case of eviction on some grounds existing before the grant or sale. Problems arise in determining what constitutes 'eviction'. Personal warrandice may be:
(1) simple warrandice, where the granter undertakes not to grant any future deed which will conflict with the right transferred;

(2) warrandice from fact and deed, where the granter undertakes that he has not granted and will not grant any such deed or do anything to conflict with that right;

(3) absolute warrandice (the usual form), where it protects the buyer from anything which conflicts with that right.

Real warrandice, now abolished, was warrandice either on the sale of land by which other land ('warrandice land') was liable to be disponed in security of the principal land or, on excambion, where one party or his heirs or assigns suffered eviction and he might have back the land which was exchanged.

warrandice clause — a clause in a deed binding the granter to a warrandice.

warrandice land — land formerly held in security for other land over which a real warrandice existed: *see* **warrandice.**

warrant — a written judicial authority, eg for service of a writ, sale, search or eviction.

warrant sale — a form of diligence for a debt by which a creditor obtains a warrant from the sheriff authorising the public sale of articles which have been poinded (qv).

warranty — an express or implied material guarantee in a contract, breach of which justifies the other party in repudiating the contract and claiming damages.

way. *See* **right of way.**

way-going crop — a crop planted on arable land in the last year of a tenancy which an outgoing tenant may take, even if the harvest postdates removing.

wayleave — a right of passage for pipes, cables and the like over heritable property, analogous to that conferred by a servitude. Unlike a servitude in the strict sense, there is no relationship of dominant and servient tenement. The right is invariably constituted by a specific contract.

Westminster Confession — a declaration of the faith and doctrine of the Church of Scotland, drawn up in 1647, entrenched in the Union Agreement of 1707 and recognised as the 'principal subordinate standard' of the Church in the Declaratory Articles scheduled to the Church of Scotland Act 1921.

whitebonnet — a person who, in collusion with a party selling by auction, attends the sale to raise the price by making offers to deceive and encourage other bidders on the understanding that he will be relieved by the seller of liability should his offer not be outbid.

Whitsunday — a quarter day in Scotland, notionally 15 May, regardless of when Whitsunday actually falls; a term day for payment of rent, although, under the Removal Terms (Scotland) Act 1886, entry to and removal from a house, agreed to take place at Whitsunday, takes place at noon on 28 May. The financial year for local authorities formerly ended on 15 May, but since 1976 it has ended on 31 March.

wilful — intentional or deliberate.

will — a deed comprising the legal expression of a person's intention as to the disposal of his property and the administration of his affairs after his death.

winding up — the process of liquidation or bringing to a close the affairs of a limited company.

without prejudice —

(1) in statutes or documents, the phrase introduces a saving clause creating an exception to the provision in which the phrase is used;

(2) in negotiations for the settlement of a dispute, the phrase, often used alone, indicates in correspondence that if the negotiations fail they are not to be founded on in later litigation.

witness —

(1) a person who gives evidence on oath in court;

(2) a person (an 'instrumentary witness') who signs a document indicating that he saw it signed by a party to the document or heard him acknowledge his signature;

(3) to sign a document as a witness.

(4) to see or hear something happen; to observe and remember.

workmen's compensation — a statutory system of compensation for employees in respect of injuries arising out of their employment, whether or not the employer was at fault. It was abolished in 1948.

writ — a legally significant writing; loosely, a court summons or petition. *See also* **initial writ.**

writ or oath — a restricted form of proof in which the pursuer can only prove his case by the production of his opponent's writings or by requiring that the case be put to his opponent on oath. *See* **oath on reference.**

Writer — a Writer to the Signet; a solicitor (obsolescent). *See* **Keeper of the Signet.**

writing — a document, whether written, typed or printed.

wrongful dismissal — a breach by an employer of the contract of employment. It is now, for practical purposes, largely superseded by statutory compensation for unfair dismissal (qv).

wrongous — wrongful.

y

yair, yare, zair *or* **zare** — a trap or cruive for fish erected across a river or bay.

year to year — the indefinite term of a contract or tenancy which will continue year after year unless and until terminated by due notice.

young person — a person aged over sixteen and under twenty-one. If found guilty of a crime or offence he may not be sent to prison but may be subject to other punishment.

z

z . . . in early Scots equivalent to 'y', eg zeir, year.

zair *or* **zare.** *See* **yair.**

PART II: EUROPEAN COMMUNITY LEGAL TERMS

a

ACP countries — African, Caribbean and Pacific countries which are parties to the Lomé Convention (qv).

absolute bar — a ground for refusing to consider the merits of a cause of action, claim or pleading in the European Court of Justice.

absolute exclusivity — the quality of an agreement (such as a licence or assignation of an industrial, commercial or intellectual property right) by which one party agrees (1) to supply goods for resale in a particular geographical area to the other party and to no other person; (2) not to compete with the other party in that area; and (3) to prevent other persons from competing with the other party. Cf **open exclusivity**.

acceleration decision — a decision speeding up the establishment of the customs union (qv) of the European Community.

accession — the admission to the European Community of a state other than a founding member (qv). *See also* **Act of Accession**.

acquis communautaire — Community patrimony; the stage in the progress of the Community towards its defined objectives, including all rights and privileges created thereby, which has been reached at any given point in time and which is presumed to be irreversible.

act adversely affecting an official or servant — an act adopted by or on behalf of a European Community institution (qv) or other body which affects (not necessarily 'adversely') the legal position of a Community official or other servant employed by that institution or body. The official or servant may seise the European Court of Justice of a dispute against his employer only where the dispute concerns such an act.

Act of Accession — an instrument of the European Community setting out the conditions upon which a state other than a founding member (qv) is admitted to the Community.

admissibility — competence; the quality of a cause of action, claim or pleading which entitles it to be heard on its merits by the European Court of Justice.

adoption — the making by an institution (qv) of the European Community of a measure having legal effect.

advance fixing — the fixing, before a transaction is entered into, of the amount of levy to be charged or refund to be allowed on the import or export of certain agricultural products (qv) under the common agricultural policy (qv) of the European Economic Community.

Advocate General — a judicial officer of the European Court of Justice to whom a case before the court is assigned, and who attends the hearing and delivers in open court an impartial reasoned opinion recommending to the court a solution to the issues of fact and law in the case.

agent — the representative of a member state or European Community institution (qv) in proceedings before the European Court of Justice.

aggregated discount — a discount granted to a buyer which is calculated by reference to the total volume sold to all buyers during a specified period, and not to the amount sold to the buyer in question during that period.

aggregation and apportionment — a system used in the European Community social security regulations of adding up the contributions made and qualifying periods completed in different member states for the purpose of acquiring and retaining the right to a benefit or determining its amount (aggregation) and then dividing the responsibility for paying the benefit between or among the member states concerned (apportionment).

agricultural product — a product subject to the common agricultural policy (qv) of the European Community, defined by Art 38(1) of the EEC Treaty as a product of the soil, stock farming or fisheries, or a product of first stage processing directly related to a product of the soil, stock farming or fisheries.

aid — assistance, whether pecuniary or in some other form, under European Community law. *See also* **state aid**.

annulment — reduction; a judicial declaration that a measure (eg of a European Community institution) otherwise having legal effect is void and thereby depriving it of legal effect.

anti-dumping — measures under European Community law against the dumping of goods (qv).

anti-dumping duty — a charge imposed under European Community law upon the importation of dumped goods.

appeal — a term occasionally (if inaccurately) used to describe proceedings for the review by the European Court of Justice of the legality of an act of a Community institution (qv), or any form of proceedings heard by that court.

appointing authority — a person or body entrusted with power to make decisions under the European Community Staff Regulations and Conditions of Employment governing the employment of officials and other servants of the Community.

apportionment. *See* **aggregation and apportionment**.

approximation of laws. *See* **harmonisation of laws**.

Assembly — the original name of the European Community institution consisting of elected representatives of the peoples of the member states, now called the European Parliament (qv).

association — a degree of integration into one or more of the fundamental principles of the European Community which falls short of accession (qv). Association applies in different ways to non-European countries and territories of several member states and to third countries or international organisations.

association agreement — an agreement concluded under Art 238 of the EEC Treaty between the European Community and a third country, a union of third countries or an international organisation, which establishes an association involving reciprocal rights and obligations, common action and special procedures.

autonomous duty — a customs tariff of the European Community fixed other than pursuant to an agreement with a third country or an international organisation.

average rate — the level of turnover equalisation taxes (qv) under European Community law calculated at a single rate deemed to correspond to the aggregate tax burden borne by domestic products where it is difficult to calculate the precise level of compensation required in the case of imports.

b

basic price — the price used to determine the level of market prices at which agricultural products (qv) covered by certain common organisations of European Economic Community agricultural markets may be sold into intervention (qv).

black clause — a clause in an agreement which causes the agreement to infringe the European Community competition rules or fall outside the scope of a block exemption (qv).

block exemption — a measure adopted by the EC Commission by authority of Art 85(3) of the EEC Treaty and EC Council regulations granting an exemption (qv) from the prohibition in Art 85(1) to certain defined categories of restrictive practices. The exemption then applies automatically to every agreement falling within the defined category of arrangements without the need for notification (qv) and individual exemption.

border tax adjustment — an adjustment under European Community law of the tax burden on imported goods comprising (1) remission of the tax imposed in the country of exportation, and (2) the imposition of a compensatory tax (qv) in the country of importation, in order to make the tax borne by the import equal to that borne by the same product when produced and consumed in the country of importation.

bracket tariff — a tariff under European Community law which, instead of prescribing a fixed amount for each item, sets upper and lower limits within which the amount applicable to each item is to be fixed by the competent authority.

C

CAP. *See* **common agricultural policy**.

CCP. *See* **common commercial policy**.

CCT. *See* **Common Customs Tariff**.

COREPER — Committee of Permanent Representatives comprising representatives of the member states of the European Community who are responsible for preparing the work of the EC Council and carrying out the tasks assigned to COREPER by the Council.

CTP. *See* **common transport policy**.

Cassis de Dijon rule. *See* **rule of reason**.

Chamber — The division in which the European Court of Justice sits when not in plenary session (qv).

charge having equivalent effect to a customs duty — any pecuniary charge, whatever its designation and mode of application, which is unilaterally imposed on goods imported into a member state of the European Community from another by reason of the fact that the goods cross a frontier.

combined nomenclature — a list of goods used to meet the requirements of the Common Customs Tariff (qv) and the external trade statistics of the European Community.

comfort letter — a letter from an official of the EC Commission stating that the Commission intends to close the file on a case involving a possible breach of European Community competition rules (qv).

Commission of the European Communities *or* **EC Commission** — an institution of the Community entrusted with ensuring the proper functioning of the Community. It combines the functions of the High Authority of the European Coal and Steel Community, the Commission of the European Economic Community and the Commission of the European Atomic Energy Community.

common agricultural policy (CAP) — the agricultural policy of the European Economic Community.

common commercial policy — the policy of the European Community with regard to trade between the European Community and third countries.

Common Customs Tariff (CCT) — the uniform tariff of customs duties applied by the member states of the European Community to imports from third countries.

common market —
(1) the form of integration between states involving the fusion of national domestic markets into one market having the characteristic of a domestic market and covering all factors of production, including goods, persons, services and capital;
(2) a term loosely used as a synonym for the European Community or its territorial area.

common organisation of agricultural markets — a legal regime applied uniformly throughout the European Community and applicable to a specified agricultural product or group of agricultural products (qv).

common transport policy (CTP) — the transport policy of the European Community.

Communities — the European Coal and Steel Community (ECSC), the European Economic Community (EEC) and the European Atomic Energy Community (EAEC or Euratom), also known as the 'European Communities' or the 'European Community'.

Community —
(1) the European Community;
(2) the territorial area of the European Community.

Community agreement — an international agreement covering matters which fall within the competence of the European Community and not of the member states.

Community institution — a body set up under, and described as such in, the founding treaties (qv) for the purpose of carrying out the tasks of the European Community, namely the European Parliament (previously, and sometimes called, 'the Assembly'), the EC Council, the EC Commission (including the former High Authority) and the European Court of Justice.

Community law — the law laid down in and derived from the treaties establishing the European Community.

Community transit — the regime governing the movement of goods through the European Community or a part of it.

compensating products — products produced by certain processes under the inward or outward processing (qv) arrangements of the European Community.

compensatory justification — a contribution by the beneficiary of a state aid (qv) to the achievement of the objectives of the European Community which is over and above the effects of the normal play of market forces and which may justify the EC Commission in exercising its discretion to allow the implementation of a proposed aid scheme.

compensatory tax — a tax imposed on imports in order to make the final tax burden on the goods the same as that imposed on domestic products.

competition —
(1) commercial rivalry; in the European Community the desired level of competition is the degree of effective competition which will enable the Community's objectives to be fulfilled;
(2) the system used to recruit officials of the European Community.

competition law — the body of rules used to enforce the competition policy of the European Community.

competition policy — the course of action adopted by the European Community in order to maintain a desired level of rivalry between commercial undertakings (qv).

competition rules — the body of rules of European Community law used to enforce competition policy.

concentration — the collection together of market power.

concerted practice — a form of co-ordination between undertakings (qv) which, without having reached the stage at which an agreement properly so-called has been reached, knowingly substitutes practical co-operation between them for the risks of competition.

Conditions of Employment — the rules governing the employment by the European Community of persons other than officials.

conjunctural policy — the policy of the European Community intended to rectify cyclical problems or short-term trends in the economy.

conscious parallelism — co-ordinated behaviour between undertakings (qv) which arises in the apparent absence of any direct or indirect contact between them.

conventional duties — customs duties fixed in accordance with an agreement concluded between the European Community and a third country or international organisation.

co-operation agreement —
(1) an agreement between the European Community and one or more third countries to co-operate in some particular field of activity;
(2) an agreement between two or more undertakings (qv) by which the parties agree to work together in some aspect of their business.

co-operation procedure — a specific procedure created by the Single European Act (qv) to which the EC Commission, the EC Council and the European Parliament must have recourse in the adoption of legislation in certain defined areas of Community competences.

co-ordination of laws. *See* **harmonisation of laws**.

Council of Europe — an international organisation comprising twenty-one member states (including the twelve member states of the European Community) responsible for drawing up conventions to which the member states may accede, notably in the fields of human rights and culture. It and its institutions are not to be confused with the European Community and its institutions.

Council of the European Communities *or* **EC Council** — a Community institution comprising representatives of the member states who are delegates of the governments of those states. It combines the functions and powers of the Special Council of Ministers of the European Coal and Steel Community, the Council of the European Economic Community and the Council of the European Atomic Energy Community. It is not to be confused with the European Council.

countervailing duty *or* **countervailing measure** — a charge or duty, usually imposed on imports, which compensates for an advantage enjoyed by the goods in question in their country of origin, such as a government subsidy granted by the exporting state, national marketing rules which favour their competitive position or fiscal measures. Cf **compensatory tax**.

Court of Auditors — a body entrusted with auditing the accounts of the European Community.

Court of Justice of the European Communities — a Community institution entrusted with ensuring that, in the interpretation and application of the founding treaties, Community law is observed. It combines the functions and powers of the Courts of Justice of the European Coal and Steel Community, the European Economic Community and the European Atomic Energy Community. It is not to be confused with the European Court of Human Rights of the Council of Europe or the International Court of Justice; consequently the term 'European Court' is ambiguous.

cumulative multi-stage turnover tax — a sales tax imposed at each transaction from production to consumption without deduction of the tax imposed at earlier taxable events.

current payment — a transfer of foreign exchange which constitutes the consideration passing within the context of an underlying transaction. Cf **movement of capital**.

customs duty — a pecuniary charge imposed on goods by reason of the fact that they are listed in a customs tariff and cross a frontier.

customs territory — a territory subject to a single customs regime.

customs union — a single customs territory defined by a common customs or common external tariff formed by merging the customs territories of several states.

d

decision —
(1) a measure adopted under Art 14 of the ECSC Treaty by the EC Commission which is binding in its entirety, ie which is generally binding on all persons;
(2) a measure adopted under Art 189 of the EEC Treaty or Art 161 of the Euratom Treaty by the EC Council or the EC Commission which is binding in its entirety, but only on those to whom it is addressed.

deflection of trade — deviation of trade from its normal course.

Deliberation Room — the room in which the judges of the European Court of Justice meet in private to discuss and vote upon cases pending before the court.

derogation — exception to a rule.

destination principle — a system under which goods are taxed in the country of consumption instead of in the country of production. The country of consumption imposes the same tax burdens on both domestic and imported products, but imposes no tax on domestic goods intended for export.

direct action — contentious legal proceedings which commence and terminate in the European Court of Justice.

direct applicability — the quality of a provision of European Community law which causes it to become law in each member state without the necessity of incorporation in or transformation into national law.

direct effect — the quality of a provision of European Community law which causes it to confer upon individuals rights which national courts must protect. 'Vertical direct effect' is occasionally used to describe cases where the right conveyed by the provision lies against a member state, and 'horizontal direct effect' is occasionally used to describe cases where the right lies against another natural or legal person.

direct taxation — taxation imposed on a legal or natural person.

directive — a measure adopted under Art 189 of the EEC Treaty or Art 161 of the Euratom Treaty by the EC Council or the EC Commission which is binding upon each member state to which it is addressed as to the result to be achieved but which leaves to the national authorities of the addressees the choice of the form and methods to be used to achieve that result. It corresponds to a recommendation under Art 14 of the ECSC Treaty.

discretionary power — power granted to a person or body to act according to his or its own judgment.

distortion — the act of changing to an unnatural form, or the condition or being so changed. Thus distortion of competition under European Community law is an unnatural change in the desired level of commercial rivalry.

division *or* scission — the operation by which the business of one legal person is transferred to more than one legal person.

domestic — (in international affairs) internal to a state.

drawback — the amount of customs duties repaid when the goods on which they are charged are exported.

dumping — the introduction of a product from one country into the commerce of another at less than its normal value.

e

EAEC. *See* **European Atomic Energy Community**.
EC Commission. *See* **Commission of the European Communities**.
EC Council. *See* **Council of the European Communities**.

ECHR. *See* **European Convention on Human Rights** *and* **European Court of Human Rights**.

ECJ. *See* **Court of Justice of the European Communities**.

ECSC. *See* **European Coal and Steel Community**.

ECSC Treaty — The Treaty of Paris 1951 (one of the three founding European Community treaties) which established the European Coal and Steel Community.

ECU. *See* **European Currency Unit**.

EEC. *See* **European Economic Community**.

EEC Treaty — one of the two Treaties of Rome 1957 (and one of the three founding treaties of the European Community), the EEC Treaty established the European Economic Community.

EFTA. *See* **European Free Trade Association**.

EMA. *See under* **European Currency Unit**.

EMS. *See* **European Monetary System**.

EUA. *See under* **European Currency Unit**.

Economic and Social Committee — a body set up under the EEC Treaty and the Euratom Treaty to advise the EC Council and the EC Commission. It consists of representatives of the various categories of economic and social activity, in particular representatives of producers, farmers, carriers, workers, dealers, craftsmen, professional occupations and the general public.

economies of scale — savings made by an undertaking which result from an increase in the size and extent of its business operations.

entry barrier — a condition that imposes higher long-run production costs on an undertaking which wishes to enter or has just entered a new market than those borne by undertakings already in the market.

equity — fairness.

equivalence — a doctrine developed by the European Court of Justice whereby national technical barriers to trade (qv) which hinder the free movement of persons or goods cannot be applied where those goods or persons conform in their country of origin to standards of production or training which, although different, are deemed to satisfy the same ends as are sought to be protected by the technical barriers.

establishment —
(1) the act of founding an organisation;
(2) the act of settling, usually on a permanent basis (*see also* **right of establishment**);
(3) an organisation, usually of a business nature, such as an agency or bank.

Euratom. *See* **European Atomic Energy Community**.

Euratom Treaty — one of the two Treaties of Rome 1957 (and one of the three founding treaties of the European Community), the Euratom Treaty established the European Atomic Energy Community.

European Atomic Energy Community (Euratom) — a community formed by several European states for the purpose of creating the conditions necessary for the speedy establishment and growth of nuclear industries.

European Coal and Steel Community (ECSC) — an economic community formed by several European states which is based on a common market, common objectives and common institutions, and which applies to the production of and trade in certain coal and steel products.

European Commission of Human Rights — An institution created by the Council of Europe (qv), comprising members equal in number to the member states of the Council, with jurisdiction to enforce the European Convention on Human Rights (qv).

European Convention on Human Rights — the Convention for the Protection of Human Rights and Fundamental Freedoms, signed in Rome in 1950, to which all member states of the Council of Europe are party. Whilst the European Community is not party to the convention, the rights enumerated in it are deemed to form a part of Community law.

European Council — regular summit meetings, convened originally outwith the framework of the Community treaties but now recognised by the Single European Act (qv), of the heads of state and government of the member states of the European Community. The European Council is not to be confused with the EC Council.

European Court of Human Rights — a court, created by the Council of Europe (qv), comprising judges equal in number to the members of the Council, with jurisdiction over the interpretation and application of the European Convention on Human Rights (qv).

European Court of Justice. *See* **Court of Justice of the European Communities**.

European Currency Unit (ECU) — a unit of value based on a basket of European Community national currencies which is used instead of a national currency for Community financial transactions, in particular in the European Monetary System and the common agricultural policy. The ECU replaced the UA (Unit of Account) or EMA (European Monetary Agreement) unit of account and the EUA (European Unit of Account).

European Economic Community (EEC) — an economic community formed by several European states which is based on a common market, common objectives and common institutions, and which applies to all matters not covered by the European Coal and Steel Community and the European Atomic Energy Community.

European Free Trade Association (EFTA) — a free trade area (qv) established in 1959 and now (1988) comprising Austria, Finland, Iceland, Norway, Sweden and Switzerland.

European Monetary System — a system of monetary co-operation between the member states of the European Community.

European Parliament — an institution of the European Community, formerly known as the 'Assembly', consisting of elected representatives of the peoples of the member states.

European political co-operation — the practice, established gradually by the member states of the European Community, and now recognised by the Single European Act (qv), of consulting in issues of foreign policy with the object of joint formulation and implementation of a common foreign policy.

exemption — a declaration from the EC Commission by authority of Art 85(3) of the EEC Treaty that the competition rules (qv) of Art 85(1) are not to apply to a particular restrictive practice or to categories of restrictive practices. *See* **block exemption**.

exhaustion of rights — the principle that an industrial or commercial property right (qv) may not be exercised in the European Community in relation to the same goods once the goods have been marketed in the Community for the first time by the holder of the right or with his consent.

export price — the price actually paid or payable for a commodity sold for export to the European Community.

external trade — trade between the European Community and third countries.

f

fiscal neutrality —
(1) the principle that taxation should not influence the conduct of business activities and the exercise of the rights and facilities granted under European Community law, which should be influenced only by objective economic factors and considerations of economic efficiency;
(2) more specifically, the principle that taxation should not discriminate on grounds of nationality or have a discriminatory effect on cross-frontier transactions.

founding member of the European Communities — one of the member states signatory to the founding treaties (namely Belgium, France, Germany, Italy, Luxembourg and the Netherlands), as distinct from those who acceded subsequently (namely Denmark, Ireland and the United Kingdom in 1973, Greece in 1981, and Spain and Portugal in 1986).

founding treaties — the three treaties which founded the European Communities, namely the ECSC Treaty (the Treaty of Paris 1951) and the EEC Treaty and the Euratom Treaty (the two Treaties of Rome 1957).

four freedoms — the freedoms provided for in the EEC Treaty, namely the free movement of goods, persons, services and capital.

free circulation — the movement of goods within the European Community which is not restricted by customs formalities, tariffs and non-tariff trade barriers. Goods from a third country are in free circulation in the Community when import formalities have been completed and any customs duties and other charges, such as charges having equivalent effect (qv), have been levied without there being any total or partial drawback (qv).

free trade agreement —
  (1) generally, an agreement between or among states to establish a free trade area (qv);
  (2) more particularly, a series of agreeements of 1972 and 1973 between the European Community and each of the member states of the European Free Trade Association (qv) establishing between them a free trade area (qv).

free trade area — the customs territories (qv) of two or more states which have granted each other reciprocal trade advantages involving the removal of customs duties and other barriers to trade upon goods produced within the area, each state remaining free to impose customs duties and other trade restrictions upon goods originating outside the free trade area.

free zone — any territorial enclave established by the member states of the European Community in order that goods in it may be considered as being outside the Community customs territory (qv).

g

GATT — The General Agreement on Tariffs and Trade, a multilateral body concerned with international commercial relations, set up by an international treaty signed in 1947. Member states of the European Community are all parties to GATT.

generalised tariff preference — the grant of tariff advantages to a range of products or to products from specified countries. *See also* **tariff preference**.

green currency — theoretical values, exchangeable not at market rates but at 'green' or representative rates, for the currencies of the member state of the European Community which are used in the administration of the common agricultural policy (qv).

guide price — the price used in some common organisations of agricultural markets in the European Community as the target price and a trigger for intervention (qv) or the imposition of import controls.

h

harmonisation of laws — the adjustment, in order to dismantle technical barriers to trade (qv), of the legislative or administrative provisions of the member states of the European Community in a given sector so that they are in accord with one another.

High Authority — an institution of the European Coal and Steel Community formerly entrusted with ensuring that the objectives of the ECSC Treaty were attained. Its powers and functions are now exercised by the EC Commission.

horizontal arrangement — an arrangement between undertakings (qv) operating at the same economic level (eg production). Cf **vertical arrangement**.

horizontal direct effect. *See* **direct effect**.

i

implement — to take further action in order to give full effect to a rule of law.

indirect taxation — taxes imposed on or borne by a product.

industrial or commercial property rights — rights such as trade marks, patents, copyright, plant breeders' rights and rights in literary or artistic property, sometimes called 'intellectual property rights'.

institution — a body set up under, and described as such in, the founding treaties (qv) for the purpose of carrying out the tasks of the European Community, namely the European Parliament (previously, and sometimes called, 'the Assembly'), the EC Council, the EC Commission (including the former High Authority) and the European Court of Justice.

intellectual property rights. *See* **industrial or commercial property rights**.

inter-brand competition — competition between products which are sold under different brands. Cf **intra-brand competition**.

interest —

(1) legal concern in a matter;

(2) money payable for the use of money lent or owed or for forbearance of a debt.

internal market — the single, uniform market within the European Community, first defined in the Single European Act (qv) as an area without internal frontiers in which the free movement of goods, persons, services and capital is ensured in accordance with the provisions of the EEC Treaty. Cf **common market.**

internal taxation — a fiscal charge forming part of a general system of taxation which applies systematically to both domestic and imported goods on the basis of the same criteria.

intervention —

(1) the active participation of national public authorities, under the direction of the European Community institutions (qv), in the control of markets through the buying in or selling of products within the common agricultural policy (qv);

(2) a procedure whereby any member state or Community institution, or a natural or legal person who can establish sufficient interest in the result, is permitted to make submissions and representations during contentious proceedings before the European Court of Justice in support of or requesting rejection of those of one of the parties.

intervention agency — a body set up by a member state of the European Community to buy in and sell agricultural products (qv) at specified prices under the common agricultural policy (qv).

intervention price — the market price at which the producer of an agricultural product (qv) may sell it to an intervention agency instead of to another buyer in the market.

intra-brand competition — competition between products which are sold under the same brand. Cf **inter-brand competition**.

intra-Community trade — trade within the European Community; trade between member states.

inward processing — customs arrangements by which goods are admitted to the customs territory (qv) of the European Community without payment of customs duties so that certain processes can be carried out in relation to the goods, after which they are exported to a third country in the form of compensating products (qv). Cf **outward processing**.

j

joint venture — an undertaking (qv) which is jointly controlled by two or more independent undertakings and which performs all the functions of a business undertaking, or is at least engaged in the production of goods or the provision of services.

jurisconsult — a jurist; a professional legal adviser.

l

legal certainty — a general principle of European Community law which requires that the application of the law to a particular situation must be reasonably predictable.

legitimate expectation — a general principle of European Community law linked to legal certainty (qv), creating a legal entitlement to anticipate the occurrence of an event which is induced by the conduct of a public authority.

liberalisation — the removal of restrictions.

linking system — a scheme by which a benefit granted by the European Community (eg the suspension of an export levy) is subject to a condition (eg that goods be purchased from an intervention agency (qv)).

Lomé Conventions — a series of association agreements (qv) now renewed every five years between the European Community on the one hand and sixty-six developing ACP countries (qv) on the other.

loyalty rebate — a discount made conditional upon a customer using only or principally a particular supplier.

m

MCA. *See* **monetary compensation amount** .

meqr. *See* **measure having equivalent effect to a quantitative restriction**.

management committee — a consultative committee with jurisdiction over a particular agricultural product (qv), which comprises representatives of the member states of the European Community and a non-voting chairman appointed by the EC Commission.

market power — the ability of a buyer or seller of particular goods or services to obtain a price that is lower or higher, as the case may be, than the normal competitive level of prices.

market share — part of the total market for particular goods or services which is held by an undertaking or group of undertakings (qv).

market sharing — the division of the market for particular goods or services between competing undertakings (qv).

measure — any legislative, judicial or administrative act adopted by a European Community institution (qv) or national authority.

measure having equivalent effect to a quantitative restriction:
(1) an encumbrance to trade which, whatever its form or description or the technique employed, has the same effect as a direct restraint, whether partial or total, on imports, exports or goods in transit;
(2) a trading rule adopted by a member state of the European Community which is capable of hindering intra-Community trade directly or indirectly, actually or potentially.

measure of constraint — an act adopted by a judicial or administrative body in a member state of the European Community which constitutes an intervention in the sphere of interest of a Community institution.

measure of instruction. *See* **preparatory inquiry**.

member state — a state which is a member of the European Communities. Depending on the context, the term may refer to:
(1) the state as a person in international law;
(2) the organs of government of the state, including the judiciary, local authorities and all persons or bodies exercising powers of a public, as opposed to a private, nature;
(3) the state and its inhabitants; or
(4) the territorial area of the state.

merger —
(1) the fusion of several European Community institutions (qv) which were created by the founding treaties and which performed similar functions (eg the replacement of the Courts of Justice of the three separate Communities by a single European Court of Justice);
(2) a transaction between two or more legal persons as a result of which either a new legal person is formed in their place or one or more of them transfers all or part of its business to the other or others.

Merger Treaty — a treaty of 1965 creating a single EC Council to take the place of the Special Council of Ministers under the ECSC Treaty and the Councils under the EEC Treaty and the Euratom Treaty, and a single EC Commission to take the place of the High Authority under the ECSC Treaty and the Commissions under the EEC Treaty and the Euratom Treaty.

MINEX — a fund similar to STABEX (qv) designed to compensate ACP countries (qv) for reductions in earnings from exports of certain minerals.

minor agreement — an anti-competitive agreement between undertakings (qv) which is not regarded as infringing the European Community competition rules (qv) because of its relatively unimportant effect on the market.

mixed agreement — an international agreement covering matters which fall partly within the competence of the European Community and partly within the competence of the member states.

monetary compensation amount (MCA) — a subsidy or levy applied to intra-Community exports or imports of an agricultural product (qv) in order to compensate for divergencies in the exchange rates of the currencies of the member states.

movement of capital — a financial operation essentially concerned with the movement of funds as such rather than for the purpose of payment or remuneration.

n

national law — the domestic law of a member state as distinct from European Community law.

negative clearance — a declaration by the EC Commission that, on the basis of the facts in its possession, a particular practice does not infringe the Community competition rules (qv).

nomenclature — a list organised on the basis of an established system of classification. Thus the nomenclature of the European Community Common Customs Tariff is a list of goods with the applicable customs duties. Cf **combined nomenclature**.

non-tariff trade barrier — a measure or practice, other than a customs tariff, which has the effect, whether direct or indirect, either of hindering the importation of goods or the sale of imported goods or of favouring the sale of domestic goods.

normal value — the comparable price actually paid or payable in the ordinary course of trade for a product which is a like product to a dumped product, when intented for consumption in the exporting country or the country of origin.

notification:
(1) service of an act or procedural document under European Community law;
(2) intimation or communication of an act;
(3) the act of submitting an agreement, decision, concerted practice or other practice to the EC Commission for the purpose of obtaining a negative clearance (qv) regarding Art 85(1) or Art 86 of the EEC Treaty or an exemption (qv) from Art 85(1).

o

objection of illegality. *See* **plea of illegality**.

observations — written or oral submissions made to the European Court of Justice where the party making them is not seeking a remedy or the vindication of a right.

official — a permanent employee of an institution (qv) of the European Community in an established post.

Official Journal — an official European Community publication containing (in the L series) the texts of regulations, directives, decisions, recommendations, agreements and other measures, and (in the C series) notices, particulars of cases brought before the European Court of Justice (with the operative part of the judgment or order) and other information. The Supplement (also known as the S series) contains notices of public contracts.

oligopoly — a market structure characterised by a small number of undertakings and a great deal of collusive or parallel conduct between them.

open exclusivity — the quality of an agreement, such as a licence or assignation of an industrial or commercial property right, by which one party agrees:
(1) to supply goods for resale in a particular geographical area to the other party and to no other person, and
(2) not to compete directly with the other party in that area;
but there is no agreement between the parties to prevent other persons from competing in the area in question. Cf **absolute exclusivity**.

operative part — the *dispositif*; that part of a judgment or order of the European Court of Justice which contains its decision. This part follows the part of the judgment or order which sets out the reasons given for the decision.

operator — someone who carries on an economic activity, such as a trader.

opinion —

(1) an act of the EC Council or EC Commission under Art 14 of the ECSC Treaty, Art 189 of the EEC Treaty or Art 161 of the Euratom Treaty, which lacks binding force;

(2) a decision of the European Court of Justice under Art 228 of the EEC Treaty as to whether an envisaged agreement is compatible with the provisions of the treaty (cf **ruling**);

(3) a decision of the European Court of Justice under Art 95 of the ECSC Treaty as to whether a proposed amendment of the treaty is compatible with Art 95;

(4) a reasoned statement made to the European Court of Justice in open court by an Advocate General recommending to the court a solution to the issues of fact and law in a case pending before it.

order for reference — an order made by a court or tribunal in a member state of the European Community in the course of proceedings pending before it, suspending those proceedings before judgment and referring to the European Court of Justice one or more questions of Community law arising on which a decision is necessary to enable the national court or tribunal to give judgment. *See also* **preliminary ruling**.

origin principle — a system under which goods are taxed only in the country of production: the tax burden is the same whether the product is manufactured for domestic consumption or for export, and no tax is imposed on goods originating in another country which are imported into the country in question.

outward processing — a customs arrangement under which goods are exported temporarily from the customs territory (qv) of the European Community with a view to being reimported subject to total or partial relief from customs duty as component parts of compensating products (qv) after they have undergone certain processing operations outside that customs territory. Cf **inward processing**.

overlapping of social security benefits — the duplication of social security benefits payable under the legislation of different member states of the European Community.

own resources — the financial resources of the European Community derived from its own revenue (levies, duties and taxes) and not from contributions made by the member states.

p

parallel import — goods imported other than through a distribution system set up by the manufacturer or an authorised distributor.

plea of illegality — a plea before the European Court of Justice that a decision of direct and individual concern to the pursuer should be annulled because the general measure from which it derives its legal effect is invalid.

plenary session — a sitting of the European Court of Justice which includes all the judges, the quorum being seven judges.

power of appraisal — the ability to carry out a subjective assessment of material facts before acting.

predatory pricing — the practice of selling below cost in order to eliminate competitors.

preliminary ruling — a decision of the European Court of Justice on a point of Community law referred to it by a court or tribunal of a member state. *See also* **order for reference**.

preparatory inquiry — an investigation, in proceedings before the European Court of Justice, into disputed matters of fact carried out after the end of the written procedure and before judgment, and involving one or more measures of instruction, such as the examination of a witness.

price competition — rivalry between different goods based on price.

primacy —
(1) generally, the prevailing effect of one system of law over another;
(2) in the Community context, that quality of Community law which gives it priority over any rule of national law with which it conflicts.

professional secrecy — a privilege based on the principle that confidential information acquired by a person in the performance of a professional or official activity must not be disclosed save where the law directs.

proportionality — a general principle of European Community law requiring that the means used to attain a given end should not exceed what is appropriate and necessary in order to achieve that end.

protective measure — a measure taken to protect the economy of a member state of the European Community from economic difficulties usually arising from external sources, such as low-priced imports.

public authority —
(1) a person or body invested with power to act of a public or state (as opposed to a private) nature;
(2) a power to act of a public or state nature.

q

qualified majority — a system of voting in the EC Council under which:
(1) the vote of each member is weighted by reference to the relative size of the member state which he represents, and
(2) a majority can be obtained only by a specified number of votes cast by a minimum number of Council members.

quantitative restriction — a measure which imposes a total or partial restraint on imports, exports or goods in transit.

quota — a restriction on the volume of trade in a particular product.

r

reasoned opinion —
(1) a statement made to the European Court of Justice in open court by an Advocate General recommending to the court a solution to the issues of fact and law in a case pending before it and giving his reasons;
(2) a document delivered by the EC Commission to a member state, before proceedings are brought against that state in the Court of Justice, setting out the reasons why and the respects in which the Commission believes the state to have failed to fulfil an obligation under the EEC Treaty or the Euratom Treaty.

recommendation —
(1) under Art 14 of the ECSC Treaty, a measure adopted by the EC Commission which is binding on the persons to whom it is addressed as to the aims to be pursued but which leaves to them the choice of the methods appropriate for achieving those aims (cf **directive**);

(2) under Art 189 of the EEC Treaty or Art 161 of the Euratom Treaty, a measure adopted by the EC Council or the EC Commission which lacks binding force.

referring court or tribunal — a court or tribunal of a member state of the European Community which makes an order for reference to the European Court of Justice for a preliminary ruling (qv).

regulation —
(1) under Art 189 of the EEC Treaty or Art 161 of the Euratom Treaty, a measure adopted by the EC Council or the EC Commission which has general application, is binding in its entirety and has direct applicability in all member states (regulations correspond to decisions under the ECSS Treaty);
(2) in reference to a member state, any measure adopted by that state of an administrative (as opposed to a legislative) nature which has general application.

relevant market — a market in competing goods and services by reference to which the economic effects of an anti-competitive arrangement are assessed.

representative rates. *See* **green currency**.

resale price maintenance — the control of the price at which the purchaser of goods may resell them to a third person.

reverse discrimination — discrimination by a member state of the European Community against one of its own nationals or against goods originating in its own territory.

right of establishment — the right of a natural or legal person to integrate himself or itself in the economy of a member state of the European Community by setting up business on the territory of that state.

rule of reason —
(1) the principle, derived from United States anti-trust law, that legislative prohibitions or certain types of commercial behaviour should not be applied literally, but only where such behaviour suppresses or destroys competition;
(2) the principle under which the prohibition imposed by Art 30 of the EEC Treaty on quantitative restrictions (qv) and measures having equivalent effect (qv) is not applied to certain types of restrictions on trade within the European Community (also known as the *Cassis de Dijon* rule).

rules of origin — rules determining the origin of goods for customs purposes.

ruling —
(1) generally, any decision of a court;
(2) a decision of the European Court of Justice under Art 103 or Art 104 of the Euratom Treaty as to whether a proposed agreement is compatible with the provisions of the treaty (*see also* **opinion**).

S

safeguard clause — a provision allowing a member state to derogate temporarily from a rule of European Community law, subject to specified conditions, in order to protect its economy. Cf **protective measure**.

scission — an operation, sometimes called 'division', by which the business of one legal person is transferred to more than one legal person.

secondary legislation — a name sometimes given to measures adopted by the institutions (qv) of the European Community under powers to act granted by one of the founding treaties (qv).

selective distribution — the distribution of goods by a supplier through intermediaries chosen by him.

Single European Act — a treaty signed in 1986 by the member states of the European Community amending and augmenting in certain respects the founding treaties (qv).

specialisation agreement — an agreement between two or more undertakings by which the parties specialise in different areas of business, eg one party concentrates on the production of certain goods and the other party ceases to produce those goods (often in order to concentrate on another area of business), obtaining its requirements from the first party instead.

specific duty — a customs duty expressed as a particular sum (eg 16 ECU) rather than as a percentage of the value of the goods.

STABEX — Stabilisation of Export Earnings; a system of financial transfers designed to compensate ACP countries (qv) in the event of a reduction in their earnings from the export of certain basic (mainly agricultural) products.

stabiliser — any mechanism adopted within the framework of the common agricultural policy (qv) which seeks to control agricultural production.

staff case — an action brought before the European Court of Justice by an official or other servant of the European Community against the employing Community institution (qv).

Staff Regulations — the regulations governing the employment of officials of the European Community.

standstill provision — a provision of European Community law which prohibits the introduction of further measures in addition to those existing at the time when the standstill provision comes into effect.

state aid — aid granted by a member state of the European Community or through state resources in any form whatever.

state trading country — a state in which trade (in particular external trade) is conducted through the agency of the state.

statement of objections — a document delivered by the EC Commission to an undertaking (qv) before the Commission reaches a decision on an alleged infringement of the European Community competition rules (qv), in which the Commission sets out the allegations which it proposes to make against the undertaking.

submissions —
(1) the opinion of an Advocate General of the European Court of Justice;
(2) the relief sought by a party to proceedings before the European Court of Justice;
(3) arguments relied on in support of a claim for relief made by a party to such proceedings.

t

target price — the price which it is hoped that producers of certain agricultural products (qv) will be able to obtain for their produce on the open market in the European Community.

TARIC — the integrated tariff, based on the combined nomenclature (qv), containing additional sub-divisions needed in order to identify goods subject to certain specific measures adopted by the European Community, such as anti-dumping duties (qv).

tariff —
(1) a customs duty;
(2) a list of customs duties (eg the Common Customs Tariff of the European Community).

tariff heading — a division of the Common Customs Tariff of the European Community under which particular goods are classified for customs purposes.

tariff preference — a tariff advantage, usually in the form of a reduced level of customs duty. *See also* **generalised tariff preference**.

technical barriers to trade — obstacles to trade derived from eg national consumer safety or environmental standards to which goods must conform.

third country — a state which is not a member state of the European Community.

threshold price — the minimum import price for certain agricultural products (qv) imported into the European Community.

transfer pricing — the practice of paying a price different from the market price or the price ordinarily payable in an arm's length transaction in the normal course of business for the supply of goods or services between associated undertakings.

transitional period —
(1) the twelve-year period, divided into three stages, during which the common market was to be established and on the expiry of which all the rules laid down in the EEC Treaty were to have entered into force and all the measures required for establishing the common market were to have been implemented;
(2) the period defined in an Act of Accession (qv) during which temporary measures apply between the date of accession and the date of the full application of the founding treaties (qv) and secondary legislation (qv) in the acceding member state (different areas of European Community law may be subject to different transitional periods of different lengths).

transnational — involving more than one country; cross-frontier.

transparent — open; easily detected; not concealed from public knowledge.

travaux préparatoires — drafts and other documents drawn up in the course of preparing the final text of a legal instrument which reflect the substance of the discussions between and the views of the persons who adopted the instrument.

Treaty of Paris. *See* **ECSC Treaty.**

Treaty of Rome. *See* **EEC Treaty; Euratom Treaty.**

turnover equalisation tax — a tax imposed on imported goods in order to make the final tax burden on them the same as that imposed on domestic goods.

turnover tax — a sales tax. *See also* **cumulative multi-stage turnover tax.**

tying — the practice of making the conclusion of a contract subject to the acceptance of supplementary obligations.

type approval — the procedure by which a member state of the European Community certifies that a type of goods satisfies the technical requirements established by Community legislation with the consequence that all models of that type of goods are deemed to satisfy those requirements.

u

undertaking —
(1) generally, a promise; an accepted obligation;
(2) generally, a natural or legal person;
(3) under Art 80 of the ECSC Treaty, a natural or legal person engaged in production in the coal or steel industry within the territories covered by the treaty and, for certain purposes, any undertaking or agency regularly engaged in distribution other than sale to domestic consumers or small craft industries;
(4) in European Community competition law, an economic unit which may consist of one or more natural or legal persons;
(5) under Art 196(b) of the Euratom Treaty, any undertaking or institution which pursues all or any of its activities in the territories of the member states within the field specified in the relevant chapter of the treaty, whatever its public or private legal status.

unit of account. *See* **European Currency Unit.**

unlimited jurisdiction — the jurisdiction of the European Court of Justice to substitute its own subjective appreciation for that of the European Community institution (qv) which adopted a measure challenged in proceedings before the court, in addition to reviewing the legality of that measure.

V

value added — wealth created by the operations of an undertaking (qv).

value added tax — a tax imposed on the amount of value added to goods or services since the preceding taxable event.

vertical arrangement — an arrangement between undertakings (qv) operating at different economic levels (eg between a manufacturer and a distributor).

vertical direct effect. *See* **direct effect**.

vertical integration — a merger between undertakings (qv) operating at different economic levels.

vested right — a right which cannot lawfully be revoked by a valid administrative measure having individual effect.